DICTATORSHIP
and
TOTALITARIANISM
Selected Readings

Edited and with an Introduction by
BETTY B. BURCH
Tufts University

D. VAN NOSTRAND COMPANY, INC.

Princeton, New Jersey

Toronto

London

New York

TO GEORGE

D. VAN NOSTRAND COMPANY, INC.
120 Alexander St., Princeton, New Jersey (*Principal office*); 24 West 40 St., New York, N.Y.
D. VAN NOSTRAND COMPANY (Canada), LTD.
25 Hollinger Rd., Toronto 16, Canada
D. VAN NOSTRAND COMPANY, LTD.
358, Kensington High Street, London, W.14, England

PREFACE

As competition between democratic and authoritarian forms of government has become increasingly acute in recent years, the study of dictatorship and authoritarianism has acquired new dimensions and greater urgency. The development of totalitarianism as a new and extreme form of authoritarianism has compounded and complicated the issue. The experiments in varying degrees of authoritarian rule by many of the newly independent, emerging countries in Asia, Africa, and Latin America have extended its scope.

The present study endeavors to provide a multi-faceted approach to the problem:

(1) While authoritarian government has manifested itself in nearly all geographic areas of the world, most studies tend to be oriented toward a particular area: totalitarianism in the communist bloc, military dictatorships in Latin America, single-party systems in Africa, and the like. The selections for this study have been chosen on a global basis. The intent is to indicate that dictatorship flourishes not in any one given set of circumstances, but in a wide variety of environments and cultures.

(2) The selections are structured on an analytical and comparative basis. The major aspects chosen for analysis are: the changing social, political, and intellectual environment; the problem of leadership; the nature and function of ideology; the role of single-party systems; and the relation of totalitarianism to the state. In each case the problem is posed and the framework set by an introduction followed by selections illustrating the different aspects or variations of the problem.

(3) To open up as many channels for insight as possible, the readings represent an interdisciplinary approach:

literary (Dostoyevsky), philosophical (Sidney Hook), psychoanalytical (Lifton), political (Brzezinski), as well as the expressions of belief and practical experience of such leaders as Mao Tse-tung, Sukarno, Khrushchev, and others. While some secondary materials are used because of their cogency in stating or analyzing the problem, much of the material consists of primary sources in the form of speeches or writings of men who have been able to put theory into practice in their particular environment.

Three terms need explanation: authoritarianism, dictatorship, and totalitarianism. As used in the introductory notes, these terms imply varying degrees of specificity. *Authoritarianism* is used as a broad, general term to cover various forms of autocratic rule in which political authority is concentrated in one man or a small group. Authoritarianism as a term connotes emphasis on obedience over individual liberty. The term may be applied to such traditional forms of government as tyrannies and despotisms as well as to both the classical and modern forms of dictatorship. *Dictatorship* is a form of authoritarian government in which power is concentrated in the hands of a single man or a small group of rulers who rule with little or no restraint. Lenin put it simply: "dictatorship is power based directly on force and unrestricted by any laws." In turn *totalitarianism* is an extreme form of dictatorship which is characterized by the unlimited and unrestrained power of the rulers, the suppression of all forms of autonomous opposition, and the atomization of society in such a way that virtually every phase of life becomes public and therefore subject to control by the state. The most obvious aspect of totalitarianism is its totalism. The selected writings and introductory notes attempt to give full and more precise insights into the meaning and manifestations of these terms.

I would like to express my gratitude to my colleagues at Tufts University for their helpful comments and to the Tufts University Faculty Research Fund.

BETTY B. BURCH

Medford, Mass.

TABLE OF CONTENTS

I

THE PROBLEM
AND THE ENVIRONMENT

The perennial question of whether man can live by bread alone has been raised with new insistence by the political phenomena of the present century. Is bread without freedom palatable? The rise of totalitarianism, and the experiments of the emerging countries with lesser degrees of authoritarianism in the name of national unity and modernization, would seem to give an affirmative answer. And yet the question remains unanswered, for even totalitarian regimes promise freedom sometimes.

The basic issues in the relation of freedom to authority are raised by Dostoyevsky in the dialogue between Christ and the Grand Inquisitor, a dialogue in which Christ remains silent. The aged Inquisitor chides Christ for offering men the freedom they dread instead of the bread they want. The Inquisitor admits that men must have something beyond bread for which to live, but whoever holds authority can guide their conscience, and whoever holds their conscience and gives them bread can rule the world and bring universal peace and happiness. The questions raised by the Grand Inquisitor lie at the heart of social organization. In contemporary terms, what price in freedom are men willing to pay for bread or higher standards of living? Does the end justify the means?

The present century has been singularly conducive to dictators, authoritarianism and utopias. Not only has the vast multiplication of population coupled with rising expectations made the question of sufficient bread acute in many areas, but the quantity and quality of rapid change in the social, political and intellectual environment have been unsettling. In times of uncertainty men turn to authority for relief.

The change in social environment has been drastic. Rural life with its simplicity and intimacy has been giving way to the complexity and anonymity of urban life, and agriculture and handicrafts are being replaced by industry and machines. Traditional cultures are shaken and shattered by the impact of modernization. As a result the individual feels helpless and alone, and he has lost his sense of belonging in an environment which seems indifferent and anonymous.

—One of the most conspicuous features of the present situation lies in the extent to which patterns of orientation which the individual can be expected to take completely for granted have disappeared. The complexity of the influences which impinge upon him has increased enormously, in many or most situtions the society does not provide him with only one socially sanctioned definition of the situation and approved pattern of behavior, but with a considerable number of possible alternatives, the order of preference between which is by no means clear. The 'burden of decision' is enormously great. In such a situation it is not surprising that large numbers of people should, to quote a recent unpublished study, be attracted to movements which can offer them 'membership in a group with a vigorous *esprit de corps* with submission to some strong authority and rigid system of belief, the individual thus finding a measure of escape from painful perplexities or from a situation of 'anomie.' [1]

One significant change in the political environment that needs emphasis has been the rise of the masses. The past century has seen the masses rise not only in numbers but also in impact on culture, values and political behavior. "—and with the mammoth trust and the mammoth trade union came the mammoth organ of opinion, the mammoth political party and, floating above them all, the mammoth state, narrowing still further the field of responsibility and action left to the individual and setting the stage for the new mass society." [2] Ortega y Gasset ex-

---

[1] Talcott Parsons, Some Sociological Aspects of the Fascist Movement, *Social Forces,* Vol. xxi, p. 140.

[2] E. H. Carr, *The New Society,* Boston, Beacon Press, p. 64.

presses the dismay of the liberal intellectual at the intrusion of the vulgar mass into positions of social and political control. Ortega is on the side of democracy, but liberal democracy rather than a mass democracy which acts only for itself and imposes on all the vulgarity of the "average" man. C. Wright Mills, however, accepts the fact of the rise of the masses, but does not see them as politically dominant. Instead he finds the masses intimidated and dominated by the 'power elite' of the big corporation, the military and the state. As the gap between the individual and the power elite is widened by the growth of mass society, the former becomes a manipulable mass to whom decisions are sold but who has no part in their making.

While Mills and Ortega differ about the role of the masses in decision making, neither questioned the increased significance of the masses in contemporary politics. Neither democracies moving from limited to universal suffrage, nor the new type of dictator balancing military with mass support, nor totalitarian regimes acting as the vanguard of the proletariat can ignore the masses. Mass propaganda, the planned manipulation of society, the creation of mass parties, the fragmentation of society with controlled mass organizations, and the atomization of the individual are but some of the responses to the rise of the masses.

The intellectual environment has changed in the past century as drastically as the social and political. Crane Brinton sketches the nature of the change. The values and beliefs of the seventeenth and eighteenth centuries, which followed hard on the heels of the Reformation in Europe, and which perhaps persist most strongly today in the United States, were self-assured, optimistic and at times even complacent. Substituting reason for faith, men were confident of their ability to make the earth a better place in which to live. Heaven on earth rather than heaven above became the goal. If the application of reason to nature could produce the fruits of science, then the application of reason to society would produce similar fruits of an ever better society. Reason and a belief in progress were the keystones of the Enlightenment, and utopia was but a short distance ahead.

The past century, however, has played havoc with these optimistic beliefs. Two world wars and continuing struggle in terms of nuclear weapons have raised doubts that society is getting better and better. More seriously, reason as a guiding force in society has come under heavy attack. A rise in anti-intellectualism followed Freud's discovery that man's actions are motivated less by reason than by emotion, less by rationality than by irrationality. Building on this premise came the science of political manipulation by propaganda and controlled communications. The attack on reason as a political factor reached its bitterest in Hitler's cynical remark that "the magnitude of a lie always contains a certain factor of credibility, since the great masses of the people in the very bottom of their hearts tend to be corrupted rather than consciously and purposely evil, and that, therefore, in view of the primitive simplicity of their minds, they more easily fall a victim to a big lie than to a little one, since they themselves lie in little things, but would be ashamed of lies that were too big."

While fascism rejected and repudiated progress through reason, communism was in the direct line of succession from the Enlightenment. Marx believed that by the application of reason to the lessons of history, i.e., scientific materialism, he had found the laws of society which would lead inevitably and inexorably to the final utopia where all men would be good and free from want. However, the rigidity of the system and the justification of means by ends made Marxism a travesty or heresy of western liberalism. Fascism, on the other hand, rejected with contempt the values of liberalism and staked its power on irrationality, violence and the glorification of the state.

Nor was the west alone in undergoing a traumatic shattering of its traditional beliefs and values. All traditional societies moving into modernization suffer from dislodgment of their value systems. Confucianism in China, as Wright points out, which for over two thousand years had laid down a pattern for maintaining harmony between man and nature and more significantly between man and society, was found to be inadequate to meet the needs of the modern world. It gave way in 1949 to communism based on struggle rather than harmony. In Asia and Africa the same unsettling process of substituting new values for old continues.

Both the rapidity and the substance of change in the social, political and intellectual environment of the individual in the twentieth century has produced bewilderment, helplessness and even despair. A widespread, though not the sole, reaction has been the search for leadership and escape into authoritarianism. "Aloneness, fear, and bewilderment remain; people cannot stand it forever. . . . The principal social avenues of escape in our time are the submission to a leader, as has happened in fascist countries, and the compulsive conforming as is prevalent in our own democracy." [3] The Grand Inquisitor spoke knowingly.

A. THE PROBLEM

— 1 —

THE BROTHERS KARAMAZOV
Fyodor Dostoyevsky*

My story is laid in Spain, in Seville, in the most terrible time of the Inquisition, when fires were lighted every day to the glory of God, and 'in the splendid *auto da fé* the wicked heretics were burnt.' Oh, of course, this was not the coming in which He will appear according to His promise at the end of time in all His heavenly glory, and which will be sudden 'as lightning flashing from east to

[3] Erich Fromm, *Escape from Freedom,* Rinehart and Co., Inc., 1941, p. 134.
* Fyodor Dostoyevsky, *The Brothers Karamazov,* The Modern Library, Random House, Inc., pp. 305-322.

west.' No, He visited His children only for a moment, and there where the flames were crackling round the heretics. In His infinite mercy He came once more among men in that human shape in which He walked among men for thirty-three years fifteen centuries ago. He came down to the 'hot pavement' of the southern town in which on the day before almost a hundred heretics had, *ad majorem gloriam Dei,* been burnt by the cardinal, the Grand Inquisitor, in a magnificent *auto da fé,* in the presence of the king, the court, the knights, the cardinals, the most charming ladies of the court, and the whole population of Seville.

"He came softly, unobserved, and yet, strange to say, everyone recognized Him. . . .

"There are cries, sobs, confusion among the people, and at that moment the cardinal himself, the Grand Inquisitor, passes by the cathedral. He is an old man, almost ninety, tall and erect, with a withered face and sunken eyes, in which there is still a gleam of light. He is not dressed in his gorgeous cardinal's robes, as he was the day before, when he was burning the enemies of the Roman Church—at that moment he was wearing his coarse, old, monk's cassock. At a distance behind him come his gloomy assistants and slaves and the 'holy guard.' He stops at the sight of the crowd and watches it from a distance. He sees everything; he sees them set the coffin down at His feet, sees the child rise up, and his face darkens. He knits his thick grey brows and his eyes gleam with a sinister fire. He holds out his finger and bids the guards take Him. And such is his power, so completely are the people cowed into submission and trembling obedience to him, that the crowd immediately make way for the guards, and in the midst of deathlike silence they lay hands on Him and lead Him away. The crowd instantly bows down to the earth, like one man, before the old inquisitor. He blesses the people in silence and passes on. The guards lead their prisoner to the close, gloomy vaulted prison in the ancient palace of the Holy Inquisition and shut Him in it. The day passes and is followed by the dark, burning 'breathless' night of Seville. The air is 'fragrant with laurel and lemon.' In the pitch darkness the iron door of the prison is suddenly opened and the Grand Inquisitor himself comes in with a light in his hand. He is alone; the door is closed at once behind him. He stands in the doorway and for a minute or two gazes into His face. At last he goes up slowly, sets the light on the table and speaks.

" 'Is it Thou? Thou?' but receiving no answer, he adds at once, 'Don't answer, be silent. What canst Thou say, indeed? I know too well what Thou wouldst say. And Thou hast no right to add anything to what Thou hadst said of old. Why, then, art Thou come to hinder us? For Thou hast come to hinder us, and Thou knowest that. But dost Thou know what will be tomorrow? I know not who Thou art and care not to know whether it is Thou or only a semblance of Him, but tomorrow I shall condemn Thee and burn Thee at the stake as the worst of heretics. And the very people who have today kissed Thy feet, tomorrow at the faintest sign from me will rush to heap up the embers of Thy fire. Knowest Thou that? Yes, maybe Thou knowest it,' he added with thoughtful penetration, never for a moment taking his eyes off the Prisoner." . . .

'The wise and dread Spirit, the spirit of self-destruction and non-existence,' the old man goes on, 'the great spirit talked with Thee in the wilderness, and we are told in the books that he "tempted" Thee. Is that so? And could anything truer be said than what he revealed to Thee in three questions and what Thou didst reject, and what in the books is called "the temptation"? . . .

" 'Judge Thyself who was right—Thou or he who questioned Thee then? Remember the first question; its meaning, in other words, was this: "Thou wouldst go into the world, and art going with empty hands, with some promise of freedom which men, in their simplicity and their natural unruliness cannot even understand, which they fear and dread—for nothing has ever been more insupportable for a man and a human society than freedom. But seest Thou these stones in this parched and barren wilderness? Turn them into bread, and mankind will run after Thee like a flock of sheep, grateful and obedient, though for ever trembling, lest Thou withdraw Thy hand and deny them Thy bread." But Thou wouldst not deprive man of freedom and didst reject the offer, thinking, what is that freedom worth, if obedience is bought with bread? Thou didst reply that man lives not by bread alone. But dost Thou know that for the sake of that earthly bread the spirit of the earth will rise up against Thee and will strive with Thee and overcome Thee, and all will follow him, crying, "Who can compare with this beast? He has given us fire from heaven!" Dost Thou know that the ages will pass, and humanity will proclaim by the lips of their sages that there is no crime, and therefore no sin; there is only hunger? "Feed men, and then ask of them virtue!" that's what they'll write on the banner, which they will raise against Thee, and with which they will destroy Thy temple. . . .

In the end they will lay their freedom at our feet, and say to us, "Make us your slaves, but feed us." They will understand themselves, at last, that freedom and bread enough for all are inconceivable together, for never, never will they be able to share between them! They will be convinced, too, that they can never be free, for they are weak, vicious, worthless and rebellious. Thou didst promise them the bread of Heaven, but, I repeat again, can it compare with earthly bread in the eyes of the weak, ever sinful and ignoble race of man? And if for the sake of the bread of Heaven thousands and tens of thousands shall follow Thee, what is to become of the millions and tens of thousands of millions of creatures who will not have the strength to forego the earthly bread for the sake of the heavenly? Or dost Thou care only for the tens of thousands of the great and strong, while the millions, numerous as the sands of the sea, who are weak but love Thee, must exist only for the sake of the great and strong? No, we care for the weak too. They are sinful and rebellious, but in the end they too will become obedient. They will marvel at us and look on us as gods, because we are ready to endure the freedom which they have found so dreadful and to rule over them—so awful it will seem to them to be free. But we shall tell them that we are Thy servants and rule them in Thy name. We shall deceive them again, for we will not let Thee come to us again. That deception will be our suffering, for we shall be forced to lie.

" 'This is the significance of the first question in the

wilderness, and this is what Thou hast rejected for the sake of that freedom which Thou hast exalted above everything. Yet in this question lies hid the great secret of this world. Choosing "bread," Thou wouldst have satisfied the universal and everlasting craving of humanity— to find some one to worship. So long as man remains free he strives for nothing so incessantly and so painfully as to find some one to worship. But man seeks to worship what is established beyond dispute, so that all men would agree at once to worship it. For these pitiful creatures are concerned not only to find what one or the other can worship, but to find something that all would believe in and worship; what is essential is that all may be *together* in it. This craving for *community* of worship is the chief misery of every man individually and of all humanity from the beginning of time. For the sake of common worship they've slain each other with the sword. They have set up gods and challenged one another. "Put away your gods and come and worship ours, or we will kill you and your gods!" And so it will be to the end of the world, even when gods disappear from the earth; they will fall down before idols just the same. Thou didst know, Thou couldst not but have known, this fundamental secret of human nature, but Thou didst reject the one infallible banner which was offered Thee to make all men bow down to Thee alone—the banner of earthly bread; and Thou has rejected it for the sake of freedom and the bread of Heaven. Behold what Thou didst further. And all again in the name of freedom! I tell Thee that man is tormented by no greater anxiety than to find some one quickly to whom he can hand over that gift of freedom with which the ill-fated creature is born. But only one who can appease their conscience can take over their freedom. In bread there was offered Thee an invincible banner; give bread, and man will worship Thee, for nothing is more certain than bread. But if some one else gains possession of his conscience—oh! then he will cast away Thy bread and follow after him who has ensnared his conscience. In that Thou wast right. For the secret of man's being is not only to live but to have something to live for. Without a stable conception of the object of life, man would not consent to go on living, and would rather destroy himself than remain on earth, though he had bread in abundance. That is true. But what happened? Instead of taking men's freedom from them, Thou didst make it greater than ever! Didst Thou forget that man prefers peace, and even death, to freedom of choice in the knowledge of good and evil? Nothing is more seductive for man than his freedom of conscience, but nothing is a greater cause of suffering. And behold, instead of giving a firm foundation for setting the conscience of man at rest forever, Thou didst choose all that is exceptional, vague and enigmatic; Thou didst choose what was utterly beyond the strength of men, acting as though Thou didst not love them at all— Thou who didst come to give Thy life for them! Instead of taking possession of men's freedom, Thou didst increase it, and burdened the spiritual kingdom of mankind with its sufferings forever. Thou didst desire man's free love, that he should follow Thee freely, enticed and taken captive by Thee. In place of the rigid ancient law, man must hereafter with free heart decide for himself what is good and what is evil, having only Thy image before him as his guide. But didst Thou not know he would at last reject even Thy image and Thy truth, if he is weighed down with the fearful burden of free choice? They will cry aloud at last that the truth is not in Thee, for they could not have been left in greater confusion and suffering than Thou hast caused, laying upon them so many cares and unanswerable problems.

" 'So that, in truth, Thou didst Thyself lay the foundation for the destruction of Thy kingdom, and no one is more to blame for it. Yet what was offered Thee? There are three powers, three powers alone, able to conquer and to hold captive forever the conscience of these impotent rebels for their happiness—those forces are miracle, mystery and authority. Thou hast rejected all three and hast set the example for doing so. . . .

We have corrected Thy work and have founded it upon *miracle, mystery* and *authority*. And men rejoiced that they were again led like sheep, and that the terrible gift that had brought them such suffering, was, at last, lifted from their hearts. Were we right teaching them this? Speak! Did we not love mankind, so meekly acknowledging their feebleness, lovingly lightening their burden, and permitting their weak nature even sin with our sanction? Why hast Thou come now to hinder us? And why dost Thou look silently and searchingly at me with Thy mild eyes? Be angry. I don't want Thy love, for I love Thee not. And what use is it for me to hide anything from Thee? Don't I know to Whom I am speaking? All that I can say is known to Thee already. And is it for me to conceal from Thee our mystery? Perhaps it is Thy will to hear it from my lips. Listen, then. We are not working with Thee, but with *him*—that is our mystery. It's long—eight centuries—since we have been on *his* side and not on Thine. Just eight centuries ago, we took from him what Thou didst reject with scorn, that last gift he offered Thee, showing Thee all the kingdoms of the earth. We took from him Rome and the sword of Caesar, and proclaimed ourselves sole rulers of the earth, though hitherto we have not been able to complete our work. But whose fault is that? Oh, the work is only beginning, but it has begun. It has long to await completion and the earth has yet much to suffer, but we shall triumph and shall be Caesars, and then we shall plan the universal happiness of man. But Thou mightest have taken even then the sword of Caesar. Why didst Thou reject that last gift? Hadst Thou accepted that last counsel of the mighty spirit, Thou wouldst have accomplished all that man seeks on earth—that is, some one to worship, some one to keep his conscience, and some means of uniting all in one unanimous and harmonious ant-heap, for the craving for universal unity is the third and last anguish of man. Mankind as a whole has always striven to organise a universal state. There have been many great nations with great histories, but the more highly they were developed the more unhappy they were, for they felt more acutely than other people the craving for worldwide union. The great conquerors, Timours and Ghenghis-Khans, whirled like hurricanes over the face of the earth striving to subdue its people, and they too were but the unconscious expression of the same craving for universal unity. Hadst Thou taken the world and Caesar's purple, Thou wouldst have founded the universal state and have given universal peace. For who can rule men if not he who holds their conscience and their bread in his hands. . . .

Thou art proud of Thine elect, but Thou hast only the elect, while we give rest to all. And besides, how many of those elect, those mighty ones who could become elect, have grown weary waiting for Thee, and have transferred and will transfer the powers of their spirit and the warmth of their heart to the other camp, and end by raising their *free* banner against Thee. Thou didst Thyself lift up that banner. But with us all will be happy and will no more rebel nor destroy one another as under Thy freedom. Oh, we shall persuade them that they will only become free when they renounce their freedom to us and submit to us. And shall we be right or shall we be lying? They will be convinced that we are right, for they will remember the horrors of slavery and confusion to which Thy freedom brought them. Freedom, free thought and science, will lead them into such straits and will bring them face to face with such marvels and insoluble mysteries that some of them, the fierce and rebellious, will destroy themselves, others, rebellious but weak, will destroy one another, while the rest, weak and unhappy, will crawl fawning to our feet and whine to us: "Yes, you were right, you alone possess His mystery, and we come back to you, save us from ourselves!". . .

The old man longed for Him to say something, however bitter and terrible. But He suddenly approached the old man in silence and softly kissed him on his bloodless aged lips. That was all his answer. The old man shuddered. His lips moved. He went to the door, opened it, and said to Him: 'Go, and come no more . . . come not at all, never, never!' And he let Him out into the dark alleys of the town. The Prisoner went away."

B. THE RISE OF THE MASSES

— 1 —

THE REVOLT OF THE MASSES
José Ortega y Gasset *

There is one fact which, whether for good or ill, is of utmost importance in the public life of Europe at the present moment. This fact is the accession of the masses to complete social power. As the masses, by definition, neither should nor can direct their own personal existence, and still less rule society in general, this fact means that actually Europe is suffering from the greatest crisis that can afflict peoples, nations, and civilisation. Such a crisis has occurred more than once in history. Its characteristics and its consequences are well known. So also is its name. It is called the rebellion of the masses. . . .

As we shall see, a characteristic of our times is the predominance, even in groups traditionally selective, of the mass and the vulgar. Thus, in the intellectual life, which of its essence requires and presupposes qualification, one can note the progressive triumph of the pseudo-intellectual, unqualified, unqualifiable, and, by their very mental texture, disqualified. Similarly, in the surviving groups of the "nobility," male and female. On the other hand, it is not rare to find to-day amongst working men, who before might be taken as the best example of what we are calling "mass," nobly disciplined minds.

There exist, then, in society, operations, activities, and functions of the most diverse order, which are of their

---

* José Ortega y Gasset, *The Revolt of the Masses*, 1932, pp. 11-18. Reprinted by permission of W. W. Norton and Co. and George Allen and Unwin, Ltd.

very nature special, and which consequently cannot be properly carried out without special gifts. For example: certain pleasures of an artistic and refined character, or again the functions of government and of political judgment in public affairs. Previously these special activities were exercised by qualified minorities, or at least by those who claimed such qualification. The mass asserted no right to intervene in them; they realised that if they wished to intervene they would necessarily have to acquire those special qualities and cease being mere mass. They recognized their place in a healthy dynamic social system.

If we now revert to the facts indicated at the start, they will appear clearly as the heralds of a changed attitude in the mass. They all indicate that the mass has decided to advance to the foreground of social life, to occupy the places, to use the instruments and to enjoy the pleasures hitherto reserved to the few. It is evident, for example, that the places were never intended for the multitude, for their dimensions are too limited, and the crowd is continuously overflowing; thus manifesting to our eyes and in the clearest manner the new phenomenon: the mass, without ceasing to be mass, is supplanting the minorities.

No one, I believe, will regret that people are to-day enjoying themselves in greater measure and numbers than before, since they have now both the desire and the means of satisfying it. The evil lies in the fact that this decision taken by the masses to assume the activities proper to the minorities is not, and cannot be, manifested solely in the domain of pleasure, but that it is a general feature of our time. Thus—to anticipate what we shall see later—I believe that the political innovations of recent times signify nothing less than the political domination of the masses. . . .

The characteristic of the hour is that the commonplace mind, knowing itself to be commonplace, has the assurance to proclaim the rights of the commonplace and to impose them wherever it will. As they say in the United States: "to be different is to be indecent." The mass crushes beneath it everything that is different, everything that is excellent, individual, qualified and select.

Anybody who is not like everybody, who does not think like everybody, runs the risk of being eliminated. And it is clear, of course, that this "everybody" is not "Everybody." "Everybody" was normally the complex unity of the mass and the divergent, specialised minorities. Nowadays, "everybody" is the mass alone. Here we have the formidable fact of our times, described without any concealment of the brutality of its features.

— 2 —

THE POWER ELITE
C. Wright Mills*

The power elite is composed of men whose positions enable them to transcend the ordinary environments of ordinary men and women; they are in positions to make decisions having major consequences. Whether they do or do not make such decisions is less important than the fact that they do occupy such pivotal positions: their failure to act, their failure to make decisions, is itself an act that is often of greater consequence than the decisions they do make. For they are in command of the major hierarchies and organizations of modern society. They rule the big corporations. They run the machinery of the state and claim its prerogatives. They direct the military establishment. They occupy the strategic command posts of the social structure, in which are now centered the effective means of the power and the wealth and the celebrity which they enjoy. . . .

Mass democracy means the struggle of powerful and large-scale interest groups and associations, which stand

* From *The Power Elite* by C. Wright Mills, pp. 3-4, 307-310.
© 1956 by Oxford University Press, Inc. Reprinted by permission.

between the big decisions that are made by state, corporation, army, and the will of the individual citizen as a member of the public. Since these middle-level associations are the citizen's major link with decision, his relation to them is of decisive importance. For it is only through them that he exercises such power as he may have.

The gap between the members and the leaders of the mass association is becoming increasingly wider. As soon as a man gets to be a leader of an association large enough to count he readily becomes lost as an instrument of that association. He does so (1) in the interests of maintaining his leading position in, or rather over, his mass association, and he does so (2) because he comes to see himself not as a mere delegate, instructed or not, of the mass association he represents, but as a member of 'an elite' composed of such men as himself. These facts, in turn, lead to (3) the big gap between the terms in which issues are debated and resolved among members of this elite, and the terms in which they are presented to the members of the various mass associations. For the decisions that are made must *take into account* those who are important—other elites—but they must be *sold* to the mass memberships.

The gap between speaker and listener, between power and public, leads less to any iron law of oligarchy than to the law of spokesmanship: as the pressure group expands, its leaders come to organize the opinions they 'represent.' So elections, as we have seen, become contests between two giant and unwieldy parties, neither of which the individual can truly feel that he influences, and neither of which is capable of winning psychologically impressive or politically decisive majorities. And, in all this, the parties are of the same general form as other mass associations.

When we say that man in the mass is without any sense of political belonging, we have in mind a political fact rather than merely a style of feeling. We have in mind (I.) a certain way of belonging (II.) to a certain kind of organization.

I. The way of belonging here implied rests upon a belief in the purposes and in the leaders of an organization, and thus enables men and women freely to be at home within it. To belong in this way is to make the human association a psychological center of one's self, to take into our conscience, deliberately and freely, its rules of conduct and its purposes, which we thus shape and which in turn shape us. We do not have this kind of belonging to any political organization.

II. The kind of organization we have in mind is a voluntary association which has three decisive characteristics: first, it is a context in which reasonable opinions may be formulated; second, it is an agency by which reasonable activities may be undertaken; and third, it is a powerful enough unit, in comparison with other organizations of power, to make a difference.

It is because they do not find available associations at once psychologically meaningful and historically effective that men often feel uneasy in their political and economic loyalties. The effective units of power are now the huge corporation, the inaccessible government, the grim military establishment. Between these, on the one hand, and the family and the small community on the other, we find no intermediate associations in which men feel secure and with which they feel powerful. There is little live political struggle. Instead, there is administration from above, and the political vacuum below. The primary publics are now either so small as to be swamped, and hence give up; or so large as to be merely another feature of the generally distant structure of power, and hence inaccessible.

Public opinion exists when people who are not in the government of a country claim the right to express political opinions freely and publicly, and the right that these opinions should influence or determine the policies, personnel, and actions of their government. In this formal sense there has been and there is a definite public opinion in the United States. And yet, with modern developments this formal right—when it does still exist as a right—does not mean what it once did. The older world of voluntary organization was as different from the world of the mass organization, as was Tom Paine's world of pamphleteering from the world of the mass media.

Since the French Revolution, conservative thinkers

have Viewed With Alarm the rise of the public, which they called the masses, or something to that effect. 'The populace is sovereign, and the tide of barbarism mounts,' wrote Gustave Le Bon. 'The divine right of the masses is about to replace the divine right of kings,' and already 'the destinies of nations are elaborated at present in the heart of the masses, and no longer in the councils of princes.' During the twentieth century, liberal and even socialist thinkers have followed suit, with more explicit reference to what we have called the society of masses. From Le Bon to Emil Lederer and Ortega y Gasset, they have held that the influence of the mass is unfortunately increasing.

But surely those who have supposed the masses to be all powerful, or at least well on their way to triumph, are wrong. In our time, as Chakhotin knew, the influence of autonomous collectivities within political life is in fact diminishing. Furthermore, such influence as they do have is guided; they must now be seen not as publics acting autonomously, but as masses manipulated at focal points into crowds of demonstrators. For as publics become masses, masses sometimes become crowds; and, in crowds, the psychical rape by the mass media is supplemented up-close by the harsh and sudden harangue. Then the people in the crowd disperse again—as atomized and submissive masses.

In all modern societies, the autonomous associations standing between the various classes and the state tend to lose their effectiveness as vehicles of reasoned opinion and instruments for the rational exertion of political will. Such associations can be deliberately broken up and thus turned into passive instruments of rule, or they can more slowly wither away from lack of use in the face of centralized means of power. But whether they are destroyed in a week, or wither in a generation, such associations are replaced in virtually every sphere of life by centralized organizations, and it is such organizations with all their new means of power that take charge of the terrorized or—as the case may be—merely intimidated, society of masses.

The institutional trends that make for a society of masses are to a considerable extent a matter of impersonal drift, but the remnants of the public are also exposed to more 'personal' and intentional forces. With the broadening of the base of politics within the context of a folk-lore of democratic decision-making, and with the increased means of mass persuasion that are available, the public of public opinion has become the object of intensive efforts to control, manage, manipulate, and increasingly intimidate.

In political, military, economic realms, power becomes, in varying degrees, uneasy before the suspected opinions of masses, and, accordingly, opinion-making becomes an accepted technique of power-holding and power-getting.

C. THE CHANGING VALUE STRUCTURE

— 1 —

IDEAS AND MEN
Crane Brinton*

In the widest terms the change in the attitude of Western men toward the universe and everything in it was the change from the Christian supernatural heaven after death to the rationalist natural heaven on this earth, now —or at least very shortly. But the clearest way of realizing the greatness of that change is to start off with a very basic modern doctrine that is unquestionably new— the doctrine of progress. . . .

The favorite explanation among the intellectuals in the eighteenth century was that progress is due to the spread of reason, to the increasing enlightenment (les

* Crane Brinton, *Ideas and Men: The Story of Western Thought*. © 1950. Reprinted by permission of Prentice-Hall, Inc., Englewood Cliffs, N. J.

lumières) that enables men to control their environment better.

Here is already seen most clearly the historic association of scientific and technological improvement with the idea of progress in the moral and cultural sense. By the eighteenth century the work of scientists from Copernicus through Newton had produced a very broad set of generalizations about the behavior of the material universe—generalizations by 1750 known to laymen at least as well as we know those of relativity and quantum mechanics. Moreover, it was clear that these Newtonian generalizations were better, truer, than those of his medieval predecessors. Still more, by mid-century there was evident the kind of material progress that is with the unreflective perhaps a much firmer source of belief in progress than is pure science. There were better roads along which coaches traveled each year a bit faster, there were obvious, homely improvements such as water closets, there was even, at the end of the century, the beginning of the conquest of the air. The conquest was an imperfect one in balloons, it is true, but even so, in 1787 a Frenchman achieved a very modern death attempting to cross the English Channel in the air. In short, a very old man in the eighteenth century might look back to his childhood as a time when men had fewer conveniences, a simpler material environment, fewer and less efficient tools and machines, a lower standard of living.

The theory of progress, however much it owes to the growth of cumulative knowledge and to the increasing ability of men to produce material wealth from their natural environment, is a theory of morals and indeed metaphysics. Men are, according to this theory, becoming better, happier, more nearly what the ideals of the best of our cultures have aimed at. If you try to pursue this notion of moral improvement into concrete details, you will come up against something of the same kind of vagueness that has always clung to Christian notions of heaven—in itself, perhaps, some evidence for the idea that the doctrine of progress is no more than a modern eschatology. Progress will lead us—and in the original, eighteenth-century notion of progress, will lead us very quickly, within a human generation or two—to a state in which men will all be happy, in which there will be no evil. This happiness is by no means just physical comfort. It is not inaccurate to say that in the eighteenth century most of those who talked of progress and the perfectibility of man were thinking in terms close to those of Christian, Greek, and later Hebraic ethics, of peace on earth to men of good will, of the absence of all the traditional vices, of the presence of the traditional virtues.

So much for the broad basis of a belief in progress on this earth. This progress was to be brought about by the spread of reason. Reason, to the ordinary man of the Enlightenment we are attempting here to follow, was the great key word to his new universe. It was reason that would lead men to understand nature (his other great key word) and by understanding nature to mold his conduct in accordance with nature, and thus avoid the vain attempts he had made under the mistaken notions of traditional Christianity and its moral and political allies to go contrary to nature. Now reason was not quite something that came suddenly into existence about 1687 (this is the date of the publication of Newton's *Philosophiae Naturalis Principia Mathematica*). It must be admitted that there were intolerant modernists who came very close to holding that everything prior to about 1700 was one huge series of mistakes, the blundering of an awkward man in a darkened room; but our average enlightened intellectual was inclined to credit the old Greeks and Romans with having done good spade work, and to believe that what we call the Renaissance and Reformation had begun once more the development of reason. It was in the Church, and especially in the medieval Catholic Church and its successors, that the enlightened found the source of darkness, the unnatural suppression of nature —in short, the Satan every religion needs. To this matter we shall return, for it is of great importance. For the moment, we can register the fact that the man of the Enlightenment believed that reason was something all men, save a few unfortunate defectives, were capable of following; reason had been suppressed, perhaps even atrophied, by the long rule of traditional Christianity. But now, in the eighteenth century, reason could once more resume its sway, and do for all men what it had done for men like Newton and Locke. Reason could show men how to control their environment and themselves.

[For] reason could show men how nature worked or would work if men ceased impeding that work by their unnatural institutions and habits. Reason could make them aware of natural laws they had in their ignorance been violating. For instance, they had been trying by tariffs, navigation acts, and all sorts of economic regulations to "protect" the trade of their own country, to secure for their country a larger share of wealth. Once they reasoned on these matters, they would see that if each man pursued his own economic interest (that is, acted naturally) to buy most cheaply and sell most dearly there would be established by the free (natural) play of supply and demand a maximum production of wealth. They would see that tariffs, and indeed all attempts to regulate economic activity by political action, made for *less* production, and could benefit only a very few who thereby got an *unnatural* monopoly . . .

The firm ground of nineteenth-century common belief in the West remained the doctrine of progress. Indeed, that doctrine in the developed cosmology seemed even firmer than in the eighteenth century. The human race was getting better, growing happier, and there was no limit to this process on earth. With some of the concrete values and standards of this process we shall shortly have to deal. Here we may note that if the tragic events of the wars and revolutions at the end of the eighteenth century suggested that progress was not uninterrupted, not a smooth and regular curve upward, in the comparative quiet from 1815 to 1914 there was plenty of material evidence to confirm the belief in some sort of progress, perhaps irregular and uneven, especially in the field of morals, but still clear progress. . . .

All over the Western world the nineteenth century sees some degree of belief in individualism, a belief that has one kind of theoretical justification and backing in the doctrine of *natural rights*. This doctrine we have seen is a very old one indeed. In the Middle Ages, for instance, natural rights were possessed by individuals, but not equally, not even absolutely, but rather as a part of the whole complex of custom and tradition in which they were brought up. Rights and reason were wedded in eighteenth-century thought, and by the end of the century the "rights of man" had become a commonplace. The concrete contents of such rights varied with the political thinker who was claiming them, but they did get codified in bills and declarations of rights, especially in the United States and in France. The Englishman of Victorian days was likely to feel that he had the rights without needing any explicit statement of them.

The essence of this concept of rights is that the individual—any and all individuals—may behave in certain ways even though other and stronger or richer individuals or groups of individuals do not want to let him behave that way. One of the groups that may not interfere with his behaving in certain ways is the powerful group we call the state. Indeed the *state* is the organized group against which the eighteenth- and nineteenth-century form of the doctrine of the rights of man is directed. The rights commonly included freedom of speech, freedom of business enterprise (usually put as "property"), often freedom of association, and, if only in the form of a right to life, at least an implied right to certain minimum standards of living. This conception of individual rights is essentially the modern equivalent of the Christian concept of the sacredness of the immortal soul in every man, the humanist conception of the dignity of man. . . .

The man of the nineteenth century had a sense of *belonging* (deeper than mere optimism) that we lack. His universe had not, as ours seems to have, got out of hand for him. He did not need to take refuge in fantastic styles or simple, often inhuman, functionalism, as we have done. He did not need to try to escape from escape. . . .

For convenience we shall classify attacks on the conventional ways of nineteenth-century life as from Right and from the Left. . . .

From these attacks there came in the twentieth century those totalitarian movements of the Right—Fascism, Nazism, Falangism, and the like—which were perhaps no more than scotched in the war of 1939. . . .

But the clearest line of antidemocratic Rightist totalitarian thought and practice comes out in the German and

Italian experience. Their nationalism, their later totalitarianism, does not prove the existence of an innate incapacity for political virtue among Germans or Italians. Their politics is a complex resultant of many historical factors. There are many variables of historical growth in the past two centuries that help explain the rise of totalitarian societies in the twentieth century in these states. We are here interested in the strands of nineteenth-century thought that helped to make Nazism and Fascism. It is true that in the nineteenth century only a few wise men recognized the direction these antidemocratic forces were taking. The very term *protofascist* for any nineteenth-century thinker is an anachronism, and therefore in a sense an injustice. Yet if we remember that human beliefs and institutions do not grow even as inevitably as an acorn into an oak, that no later stage is an inevitable consequence of an earlier, the search for totalitarian origins in the nineteenth century will not mislead us.

One strand is certainly the simple strand of historical nationalism we have already noted as universal in the West. To this must be added, especially for Germany, a very strong strand of "racism," the notion that Germans are biologically a special variety of *homo sapiens*—blond, sturdy, clean-cut, virtuous, the destined master race. To outsiders, this is clearly an example of a social myth; the Germans aren't even in a majority blonds. But we today are pretty well used to myths which, though they do not correspond to scientifically established truth, clearly influence people and get them to work together. The irony has often been pointed out: The first strong modern literary source of these ideas of Germanic caste and color lies in the writings of a nineteenth-century Frenchman, the Comte de Gobineau. Actually there is a long history in the West of prestige attached, if not to actual blondness, at least to lightness of color. Even among the ancient Greeks, legend made such gods as Apollo blond; the whole Hindu caste system depends on *varna,* color; even in the Christian artistic tradition you will note a certain tendency to make the saints rather more blond than the sinners. Scientifically speaking, we do not know whether or not blonds tend to be more virtuous than brunettes; the question is simply meaningless. It is, however, a fact that this and other beliefs of a similar sort entered into the antidemocratic faith of the Nazis. As early as 1842, a German historian could write:

> The Celtic race, as it has developed in Ireland and in France, has always been moved by a bestial instinct, whereas we Germans never act save under the impulsion of thoughts and aspirations which are truly sacred.

The American historian of the revolt of the Netherlands, Motley, could contrast Celtic "dissoluteness" and German "chastity."

A third strand, and probably in fact the strongest and most important in Nazism and Fascism alike, is the emphasis on the authority of a ruler and a small group of the party elite around the ruler. This concept too has firm nineteenth-century background, and indeed is in one sense merely a reappearance of very old notions like that of the divine right of kings. Perhaps there is no better nineteenth-century proto-fascist than the once-respected Victorian writer Thomas Carlyle, whose *Heroes and Hero-worship, Shooting Niagara, Nigger Question* are full of the leadership principle, the necessity of the stupid many's subservience to the wise few, the need of permanence, status, subordination in our madly and stupidly competitive society. . . .

Very broadly, we may say that nineteenth-century attacks from the Left on what the Victorian compromise had made of the ideals of the Enlightenment bore as their gist the broadening out of political democracy into social and above all economic democracy. The formula is a simplification. Men on the Left had as much trouble with the eternal tension between the ideals of liberty and authority as did men on the Center. . . . The differences between the modified democratic way of life, cosmology, culture, or even religion represented by contemporary Leftist trends in the West and the orthodox Marxist position are very great indeed; here we can but indicate some of the main lines an analysis of these differences should take. But first it must be said that both the Marxist and the non-Marxist Left can fairly claim common origin in the Enlightenment, and that both are in important ways opposed to traditional Christianity. Both reject the doctrine of original sin in favor of a basically optimistic view of human nature, both exclude the supernatural, both focus on the ideal of a happy life on this earth for everyone, both reject the ideal of a stratified society with permanent inequalities of status and great inequalities of income. It is only fair to note that today it is possible for a non-Marxist Leftist to accept some measure of traditional Christian pessimism, and indeed to consider himself a Christian. Marxism, a much more rigid creed, can hardly make any open compromise with Christianity or any theistic religion, but must remain firmly positivist and materialist.

Indeed, this rigidity of doctrine is one of the main differences between the two systems of belief. The democratic Leftist retains at his most collectivist at least a minimum of the old liberal belief that there must be intellectual freedom to entertain new ideas, to experiment, to invent. Even when he is no longer moved by a feeling for "rights" of the individual, he is committed to the notion of progress through variation, and he knows that groups as such do not have new ideas. You can tell much from the tags and clichés that even the intellectuals cannot quite avoid; the democratic Leftist will still hold that the only dogma is that there be no dogmas, or that the only room for intolerance is for intolerance of the intolerant. . . .

The democratic Leftist retains always, even in his most up-to-date form, something of the old distrust of any system of ideas that tries to sink the individual in the group, that seems to make the individual merely a cell of an all-important whole; he preserves at bottom a genuine respect for a great deal of the apparatus of individual rights which, especially as they apply to property, he is likely to dismiss rather cavalierly in some of his moods; he does not believe in the inevitability of the class struggle and of revolution and hopes that he can attain greater social and economic equality, greater stability in society, better administration both in business and government, by a process of voluntary change effected through legislation put through in the usual democratic way; he is, in modern cant terms, a gradualist and a reformist; he is, especially in recent years, increasingly willing to pay some attention to critics of the basic ideas of the Enlightenment, critics of the sort we have here classed as attackers from the Right, and critics of the kind we shall study in the next chapter as anti-intellectuals; and, having observed the totalitarian societies of the Nazis, the Fascists, and the Russian Communists in our own time, he has come to conclude that uniformity, regimentation and absolute authority are prices much too great to pay for order and security from the whirl of Western competitive society.

We come at last to Marxist socialism, or communism. From our point of view, Marxism—or Marx-Lenin-Stalinism, to give the canonical succession—is a very rigorous development of, or heresy of, the world-attitude of the Enlightenment. It stands toward the central democratic form of the Enlightenment in some ways as Calvinism stands toward traditional Christianity of the Roman Catholics, or perhaps better, toward the Anglicans who under one formal church organization run the spectrum of belief from unitarianism to high sacramentalism. Marxism is a rigorous, dogmatic, puritanical, determinist, firmly disciplined sect of eighteenth-century optimistic humanitarian materialists. . . .

The ideal, the end, of Marxism is the philosophical anarchism among free and equal human beings that is one of the persistent themes of the Enlightenment.

The means, however, is violent revolution and a transitional state of dictatorship in which there will be rigorous use of authority from above, a strict discipline among the masses, the whole apparatus of a totalitarian society. Here Marxism breaks sharply with the tradition of the Enlightenment, which, though proud of revolutions like the American and the French, was also a bit ashamed of the tar and feathering and guillotining, and regarded political revolution as at best a necessary evil to be avoided if possible. Now in this world the means affects the end. So far, the Marxist effort to arrive at anarchy by the use of authority has not got beyond a very firm use of authority by a small ruling class. . . .

There is a center—not a dead center—in the nineteenth century, which we have called the Victorian compromise. That compromise sought to retain a moderate political democracy, a moderate nationalism, and great individual economic freedom of enterprise balanced by a strict moral code and conventional, churchgoing Christianity. In a Western society based on that compromise there was great industrial and scientific advance, great material inequalities and yet for the lower classes a higher standard of living in a material way than ever before, and a lively and varied intellectual and artistic flourishing.

Yet this intellectual and artistic flourishing, if contrasted with that of the thirteenth century, or of fifth-century Athens, lacked unity of style, perhaps unity of purpose. For the nineteenth century was a time of extraordinary diversity of thought, an age of multanimity. Its extremes were great extremes, its tensions clearly marked—tradition against innovation, authority against liberty, faith in God against faith in the machine, loyalty to the nation against loyalty to humanity—the list could be very long indeed. Somehow the nineteenth century managed to keep these warring human aspirations, these basically conflicting ideals of the good life, in uneasy balance. Our century has seen this balance upset. Two great wars and a great depression are the witnesses of this upset. We are now attempting, among ideals quite as conflicting as those of the nineteenth century—they are indeed essentially the same ideals—to establish a balance of our own. . . .

It seems safer here to treat anti-intellectualism, especially in its bearing on the study of men in society, as simply one of the characteristic manifestations of the spirit of our age. . . .

Freud's contribution to contemporary anti-intellectualism was very great. His work, taken with that of Pavlov and many other psychologists and physiologists, put great emphasis on the proportion of human actions in which the traditional instrument of thought—Aristotle's *phronesis,* Christian *ratio,* the reason of Locke and the Encyclopedists, even the illative sense of Newman—had no part, or little part. Action came to the anti-intellectual to be the result of automatic responses, natural or conditioned, of all sorts of unconscious drives and urges, of traditions, social habits, even theological and metaphysical principles made by early training and conditioning part of the individual's way of responding to the need to make a decision. To the anti-intellectual actual ratiocinative thought in an individual is to the rest of his living even less than the small part of the iceberg visible above water is to the whole mass of the iceberg. The *amount* of reasoning in human life, then, and not the *existence* of reasoning, is the point over which the anti-intellectual and those who oppose anti-intellectualism really differ. . . .

Much of modern anti-intellectualism, unpalatable though it is to optimistic democratic taste, is actually widespread in Western culture today. Even semantics has spread into popular consciousness, to be sure in forms Korzybski would hardly recognize. We have all heard about rationalization, propaganda, the ambiguities and other inadequacies of language; we are all reminded daily that to get ahead in this world you must exercise your skill in handling other people, you must deliberately win friends and influence people by arts other than logic. The experts in propaganda know that one of the factors they must reckon with is public awareness and distrust of propaganda, which the French call expressively—and cynically—*bourrage de crâne,* "brain-stuffing."

We are brought squarely up against the problem of the relation of anti-intellectualism to our democratic tradition, way of life, cosmology. Democracy as it ripened in the eighteenth century held out hope of rapid and thorough social change toward universal happiness on earth to be achieved by educating all men to use their natural reason —or at least by entrusting power to an enlightened group of political planners who could devise and run institutions under which all men would be happy. Anti-intellectualism maintains against these democratic beliefs the belief that men are not and cannot under the best educational system be guided by their reason, that the drives, habits, conditioned reflexes that mostly do guide them cannot be changed rapidly, that, in short, there is something in the nature of man that makes him and will continue to make him behave in the immediate future not very differently from the way he has behaved in the past.

— 2 —

STRUGGLE VS. HARMONY: SYMBOLS OF COMPETING VALUES IN MODERN CHINA
Arthur F. Wright [*]

Traditional China was characterized by a remarkable homogeneity of mores, institutions, and values. In this it resembled the simpler societies in which, as MacIver has pointed out, the institutions are in broad accord with the mores, and one system of values prevails, being reaffirmed in every aspect of life. During the past hundred years, China's perdurable synthesis of doctrines and institutions has been slowly but certainly undermined. While the impact of the Western powers and Western technology forced the modification of Chinese institutions, the subtle penetration of Western ideas altered or destroyed every long-accepted value. The past century of China's history can be seen as a continuous struggle to regain its ancient homogeneity. That century is marked by repeated attempts to create groups of modified institutions to meet the challenge of Western power, together with groups of modified values which, it was hoped, would support the new institutions, and check the spread of divisive Western ideas. These efforts failed, and with each failure more and more traditional institutions and values were abandoned as incapable of existing in amalgam with Western elements. In this process, different social groups reacted differently to the persisting appeal of the old and the attrac-

* Arthur F. Wright, "Struggle vs. Harmony: Symbols of Competing Values in Modern China," *World Politics,* Vol. VI, October 1953, pp. 31-38. Reprinted by permission.

tion of the new and, in so reacting, further undermined the old synthesis of values and institutions.

Chinese Communists, in their bid for power, played upon Chinese longings for a community-wide synthesis of values and institutions; they suggested that Marxism-Leninism alone offered a basis on which such a synthesis could be created. They reinforced this appeal by claiming for a Communist order the same universality that Chinese had for centuries claimed for their Confucian synthesis of institutions and values. Yet for a Chinese to respond to these appeals meant the rejection of every time-honored value of Chinese society and the institutions with which they were associated. The Chinese Communist consolidation of power has brought with it the overthrow of the traditional social order centering on the family; it has brought a large-scale redistribution of status, a large number of new institutions both social and governmental. To justify and sanction this complex of radical innovations, the Communists have simultaneously attacked older values and the survivals of older institutions and have sought to inculcate new values which will support the new system.

It may throw some light on this process to consider the Communist effort to replace a value that was central to China's traditional order—Harmony—with a value that is essential to all Communist systems—Struggle. I shall deal first with the traditional value as a tenet of Confucian faith and as an ingredient of various attempted ideological syntheses in pre-Communist China. I shall then attempt to analyze the value of struggle as it is propounded in Chinese Communist writings, showing the various ways in which it is rationalized and promoted as a new, central, social and political value.

Obviously, we cannot isolate either of these competing values or their symbols from the context of symbolized values of which they are each a part. Thus, for example, the traditional value of harmony is expressed in various behavioral norms—care for "face," reliance on a sense of humor, esteem for compromise as a means of resolving conflicts of interests, etc. Struggle, on the other hand, must be understood in the context of Marxist-Leninist attitudes and thought. It is inseparably bound up with the idea of class status and class struggle; it is essential to a dialectical view of human history and human affairs; it is closely related to the messianic vision of the Communist, who sees himself as fighting a war for the liberation of mankind.

A classic statement of the value of harmony is found in the Confucian canonical treatise, *The Doctrine of the Mean*. This statement has been called "a summary of the Confucian doctrine," and its words have been graven on the minds and hearts of educated Chinese for many centuries:

> While there are not stirrings of pleasure, anger, sorrow, or joy, the mind may be said to be in a state of EQUILIBRIUM. When these feelings have been stirred and they act in their due degree, there ensues what may be called the state of HARMONY. This EQUILIBRIUM is the great root (from which grow all the human actions) in the world, and this *HARMONY* is the universal path (which they all should pursue). Let the states of equilibrium and harmony exist in perfection, and a happy order will prevail throughout heaven and earth, and all things will be nourished and flourish.

Note that in this statement harmony (*ho*) and equilibrium (*chung*) are regarded as the great norms of both the natural and the human worlds. Nature, in Chinese thought, was not an environment which man forcibly subdued, but an organism of whose governing principle man should become aware so that he might live in harmony with it. No Chinese artist or writer could share or even comprehend the pre-Romantic Western antipathy to nature; they would have been astounded at the view, expressed as late as the eighteenth century, that mountains were "effroyables, païennes, diaboliques." Nature was seen as animated by a harmonious and harmonizing energy; man could learn from nature not only how to live serenely with nature but also how to live in harmony with himself and his fellow men.

For the individual, a harmonious adjustment to social mores and institutions was held to be the ultimate in self-cultivation, and, at the same time, a contribution to the goal of a harmonious society.

No lure is greater than to possess what others want,
No disaster greater than not to be content with what one has,

No presage of evil greater than that men should be wanting to get more.
Truly: "He who has once known the contentment that comes simply through being content, will never again be otherwise than contented."

In poetry, in folk tales, in histories and essays, in drama and the novel, the value of harmony in social relations has been ceaselessly reiterated. And this value is expressed, as it is sustained, by a willingness to compromise, by the proper display of humility, by a concern for the status and reputation of others, by a reluctance to enter into doctrinal or legal controversies. Abundant evidence of the pervasiveness and importance of the value of harmony in traditional China is to be found in the recurrence of the symbols of harmony in innumerable era names, place names, personal names, street, palace, temple, and studio names throughout Chinese history. . . .

It was against a background of its rivals' repeated failures to bring about a synthesis of values and institutions that the Communist Party rose to power. It is significant that Ch'en Tu-hsiu, the co-founder of the Chinese Communist Party, should have been the first to renounce Chinese institutions and values in their entirety. He reacted against the group of values centering on the value of harmony—which he felt impaired China's ability to adjust to the modern world—and embraced the nineteenth-century European cult of the dynamic, going so far as to declare that "war is to society what movement is to the body." In taking his stand he cried, "The Oriental peoples may regard all this as madness, but in what condition do all these Oriental people, with their love of peace, quiet and harmony, now find themselves?"

In the years following the foundation of the Chinese Communist Party in 1921 Marxist-Leninist ideas had an ever-widening influence on the intellectuals. Just as, a generation before, the ideas and terminology of Darwin and Huxley had become the common coin of intellectual discourse, so now "class struggle," "the dialectic," and the Marxist ideas of the "stages" of society pervaded academic and literary discourse. This is not the place to describe the rising tide of Marxist thought, but we should note that it resulted in a further attrition of traditional values and won the support of some, the consent of others, to the subsequent effort of the Chinese Communist Party to impose its synthesis of institutions and values on the Chinese people as a whole. . . .

Class struggle as the dominant motif in human relations and the dynamic in the growth of society is of course insisted upon by all the ideologues. A high degree of class consciousness, commitment to the proletariat in the class struggle, and proficiency in "class analysis" of every human situation are demanded of all true believers. It need hardly be said that to accept this complex of ideas means the utter repudiation of the old Chinese ideal of two mutually supporting and mutually dependent classes—the governors and the governed—dwelling in harmony and in a common commitment to state and culture.

II

LEADERSHIP

Every form of political organization involves some system of leadership, some system for decision-making. A basic question, however, is whether certain individuals by the nature of their personal endowment make history or whether, on the contrary, the actions of individuals are determined by their environment. The former leads to the theory of the hero in history and the latter to social determinism. Both theories have served as the basis for authoritarian regimes.

Thomas Carlyle believed that some men rise above the level of the masses because of their special and superior qualities and consequently would be outstanding at any time and in any situation. His belief that the superior man should be given power to rule was easily adapted by Hitler to his theory of the man of fate destined to rule. On the other hand, Karl Marx was a social determinist. He maintained that the course of history is fixed by the mode of production which operates independently of man's will. It is the material conditions which determine the ideas and institutions of men at any given period of history, and not the contrary.

Theories of history for the most part avoid the extreme of the individual or environment as sole determinant of history, but give varying weight to each. Sidney Hook points out that while some events are inevitable (America would sooner or later have been discovered without Columbus), at certain times in history a cluster of events arises which presents an opportunity for choice. It is here that a given individual may act so as to push history in one direction rather than another. He believes that Lenin was such a man at such a time. Speaking of the Russian revolution of 1917, he says: "But from first to last it was Lenin. Without him, there would have been no October Revolution." [1] Plekhanov, a contemporary of Lenin and a Marxist, represents the orthodox communist view which admits the role of men as semi-determinant but places greater emphasis than Hook on social determinism. Some events are subject to human decision, but these can be only minor events in the main inevitable stream of history. "Owing to the specific qualities of their minds and characters, influential individuals can change the *individual features of events and some of their particular consequences,* but they cannot change their general *trend,* which is determined by other forces. . . ." [2]

Another preliminary problem of leadership is the difficulty of pin-pointing the exact locus of decision-making power. In democracies as well as authoritarian regimes decisions are made by the few rather than the many. Michels in his "iron law of oligarchy" postulates that any *rational* organization, including the democratic state, gives power to only a few. "Who says organization says oligarchy." This rule applies more obviously to authoritarian states. While it is true that in such regimes there must be some diffusion of power since no dictator or ruling elite can make all the decisions, nevertheless such elite can make basic decisions with fewer outside restraints than in a democracy. Communist theory provides for a dictatorship of the proletariat, but the Communist party acts as its vanguard, presumably making the decisions that the proletariat would make if it knew better. In fact, however, decisions are made not by the party as such, but by a top elite who merely transmit their decisions through the party organization to the masses. Khrushchev may have based his posthumous attack on Stalin on the latter's violation of Lenin's principle of "collective leadership," but the question remains as to how collective is leadership under Khrushchev.

A conspicuous aspect of the political scene in recent

[1] Sidney Hook, *The Hero in History,* Beacon Press, 1957, p. 203.

[2] George Plekhanov, *The Role of the Individual in History,* International Publishers, 1940, p. 48.

years has been the increase in authoritarian regimes under the guidance of a new type of ruling elite. The traditional leader interested primarily in maintaining the status quo is not obsolete, but the new leaders are usually intellectuals, representing a new alignment with the masses, and concerned with the process of change in the form of independence movements, modernization programs, or enactment of ideological blueprints. While the phenomenon is widespread, it is particularly prevalent in emerging countries. "The gestation, birth, and continuing life of the new states of Asia and Africa, through all their vicissitudes, are in large measure the work of intellectuals. In no state-formation in all of human history have intellectuals played such a role as they have in these events of the present century." [3] While variations among the new ruling elite are numerous, certain patterns of leadership may be distinguished. Power may rest in the hands of an individual leader, a party elite, or an army elite.

The individual leader or dictator has been historically the most numerous of the above patterns. A dictator may be simply the traditional strong man who rules as long as he controls the use of force, or he may be the new type who maintains power by balancing army and mass support, or he may rule by charisma. Max Weber describes the charismatic leader as one who believes that he is a man of destiny fulfilling a "divine mission," and who is able to impart fanatic faith in his mission to others. The charismatic leader plays a new and significant role in states which have won independence from colonial rule but have not yet achieved national unity. Here the charisma of the leader holds together the diverse elements of the state and personifies the "nation" until such a time as national unity can be achieved. However, dictators, whether charismatic or strong men on horseback, have rarely been able to provide for orderly succession without a disruptive power struggle such as took place after the death of both Lenin and Stalin.

Rule by the elite of single, authoritarian parties is a more recent phenomenon. While various patterns of the

[3] Edward Shils, "The Intellectuals in the Political Development of the New States," *World Politics,* Vol. XII, No. 3 (April 1960), p. 329.

one-party system have recently emerged, the Communist party in many respects has by now become the classical type. The party as leader or vanguard of the proletariat was a major contribution of Lenin to communist theory and practice. Marx had given the party the limited role of arousing the proletariat to class-consciousness, after which he believed that the working class would spontaneously arise against its exploiters. Lenin, however, doubted the ability of the proletariat to move beyond mere trade-union consciousness and spontaneously to throw off its chains, especially in the face of Czarist police repression. It was necessary, therefore, to have a conspiratorial, highly elitist party to prepare for the revolution and to lead the proletariat through it. Once in power Lenin and his successors extended the role of the vanguard beyond the point of the anti-capitalist revolution. Now, as Trotsky put it, there was to be a permanent or continuous revolution led by the party through the stages of the dictatorship of the proletariat and socialism to the final goal of communism where each would receive according to his need and "pre-history" would cease. Short of the final goal, absolute power must be concentrated in the party or, more precisely, in the party elite to keep the revolution moving and prepare the necessary pre-conditions for communism. The concept of the infallible party as guardian and sole purveyor of the true ideology, all opposition to which must be rooted out as heresy and treachery, is perhaps understandably the one aspect of doctrine on which all national communist parties are the most staunchly and unequivocally agreed.

The communist party, unlike the all-inclusive membership of some African single parties, is by doctrine essentially selective or elitist. It must therefore select its members with great care, determine the most effective size, and lay down qualifications for continued good standing in the party. Ch'en Yün describes the qualities of an ideal party member. More serious to the party is the problem of keeping its members ideologically pure, cohesive, disciplined and continuously and enthusiastically active. Liu Shao ch'i indicates this fear of inner contamination and advocates intra-party struggles to preserve purity and dynamism. The ultimate device is the periodic purge of membership. It is, of course, the inner party elite who determines what constitutes ideological purity and enforces its standards within the party. This produces a not undesirable insecurity among the party rank and file but flexibility of action for the party leaders.

The army as leader is not a new phenomenon as the long history of *"caudilloism"* or military rule in Latin America indicates. In its traditional form an army officer, or group of officers, seized power by a *coup d'état,* established a military dictator or *"junta,"* and endeavored to maintain the status quo. This simple form is giving way in contemporary conditions to a more complex form which is based on popular mass support rather than limited segments of the society such as landowners and clergy, and which broadens its objectives from the status quo to social change. While simple lust for power is not always lacking, as Lieuwen indicates, army rule is being increasingly used in developing areas as the most efficient means for achieving rapid modernization. In states lacking national consciousness or ruled by reactionary and frequently rapacious groups, the army is often the most cohesive group in the society because of its *esprit de corps,* and, according to Pye, the most modern-minded as the result of its training with modern weapons, organization and outside contacts. In such circumstances army leaders, disillusioned with the corruption or incompetence of the traditional rulers or the inefficiency of experiments with pseudo-democratic devices, seize power and rule in order to achieve the social change necessary for modernization. The objective of social change may be democratic but the method is authoritarian, and consequently the classification of army regimes as democratic or dictatorial is difficult.

A. THE PROBLEM: HERO OR ENVIRONMENT?

— 1 —

ON HEROES, HERO-WORSHIP AND THE HEROIC IN HISTORY
Thomas Carlyle*

—so, by much stronger reason, may I say here, that the finding of your *Ableman* and getting him invested with the *symbols of ability,* with dignity, worship (*worth*-ship), royalty, kinghood, or whatever we call it, so that *he* may actually have room to guide according to his faculty of doing it,—is the business, well or ill accomplished, of all social procedure whatsoever in this world! Hustings-speeches, Parliamentary motions, Reform Bills, French Revolutions, all mean at heart this; or else nothing. Find in any country the Ablest Man that exists there; raise *him* to the supreme place, and loyally reverence him: you have a perfect government for that country; no ballot-box, parliamentary eloquence, voting, constitution-building, or other machinery whatsoever can improve it a whit. It is in the perfect state; an ideal country. The Ablest Man; he means also the truest-hearted, justest, the Noblest Man; what he *tells us to do* must be precisely the wisest, fittest, that we could anywhere or anyhow learn; —the thing which it will in all ways behoove us, with right loyal thankfulness, and nothing doubting, to do! Our *doing* and life were then, so far as government could regulate it, well regulated; that were the ideal of constitutions.

* Thomas Carlyle, *On Heroes, Hero-Worship and the Heroic in History*. Lecture delivered in 1840. A. L. Burt Company, n.d.

— 2 —

A CONTRIBUTION TO THE CRITIQUE OF POLITICAL ECONOMY
Karl Marx*

The general conclusion at which I arrived and which, once reached, continued to serve as the leading thread in my studies, may be briefly summed up as follows: In the social production which men carry on they enter into definite relations that are indispensable and independent of their will; these relations of production correspond to a definite stage of development of their material powers of production. The sum total of these relations of production constitutes the economic structure of society—the real foundation, on which rise legal and political super-structures and to which correspond definite forms of social consciousness. The mode of production in material life determines the general character of the social, political and spiritual processes of life. It is not the consciousness of men that determines their existence, but, on the contrary, their social existence determines their consciousness. At a certain stage of their development, the material forces of production in society come in conflict with the existing relations of production, or—what is but a legal expression for the same thing—with the property relations within which they had been at work before. From forms of development of the forces of production these relations

* Karl Marx, *A Contribution to the Critique of Political Economy,* The International Library Publishing Co., New York, 1904, pp. 11-13.

turn into their fetters. Then comes the period of social revolution. With the change of the economic foundation the entire immense superstructure is more or less rapidly transformed. In considering such transformations the distinction should always be made between the material transformation of the economic conditions of production which can be determined with the precision of natural science, and the legal, political, religious, aesthetic or philosophic—in short, ideological forms in which men become conscious of this conflict and fight it out. Just as our opinion of an individual is not based on what he thinks of himself, so can we not judge of such a period of transformation by its own consciousness; on the contrary, this consciousness must rather be explained from the contradictions of material life, from the existing conflict between the social forces of production and the relations of production. No social order ever disappears before all the productive forces, for which there is room in it, have been developed; and new higher relations of production never appear before the material conditions of their existence have matured in the womb of the old society. Therefore, mankind always takes up only such problems as it can solve; since, looking at the matter more closely, we will always find that the problem itself arises only when the material conditions necessary for its solution already exist or are at least in the process of formation. In broad outlines we can designate the Asiatic, the ancient, the feudal, and the modern bourgeois methods of production as so many epochs in the progress of the economic formation of society. The bourgeois relations of production are the last antagonistic form of the social process of production—antagonistic not in the sense of individual antagonism, but of one arising from conditions surrounding the life of individuals in society; at the same time the productive forces developing in the womb of bourgeois society create the material conditions for the solution of that antagonism. This social formation constitutes, therefore, the closing chapter of the prehistoric stage of human society.

— 3 —

THE HERO IN HISTORY
Sidney Hook*

There is a perennial interest in heroes even when we outgrow the hero worship of youth. The sources of this interest are many and deep. But they vary in intensity and character from one historic period to another. In our own times interest in the words and acts of outstanding individuals has flared up to a point never reached before. The special reasons for this passionate concern in the ideas and deeds of the uncrowned heroes of our age are quite apparent. During a period of wars and revolutions, the fate of peoples seems to hang visibly on what one person, perhaps a few, decide. It is true that these special reasons reflect the dramatic immediacy of issues joined in battle, but there are other sources of interest which operate in less agonized times. We shall discuss both.

1. The basic fact that provides the material for interest in heroes is the indispensability of *leadership* in all social life, and in every major form of social organization. The controls over leadership, whether open or hidden, differ from society to society, but leaders are always at hand— not merely as conspicuous symbols of state, but as centers of responsibility, decision, and action. There is a natural tendency to associate the leader with the results achieved under his leadership even when these achievements, good or bad, have resulted despite his leadership rather than because of it. Where many factors are at work, the fallacy of *post hoc, ergo propter hoc* has a fateful plausibility to

* Sidney Hook, *The Hero in History* (Boston: Beacon Press, reprinted by arrangement with Humanities Press, 1955), pp. 1-19, 103-116, 169-170. Reprinted by permission.

the simple mental economy of the uncritical multitude as well as to impatient men of action. A Hoover will be held accountable for a depression whose seeds were planted long before his advent. A Baldwin will be considered safe and sane if no social catastrophe breaks out during his ministry, even if he has lit a slow-burning fuse to the European powder magazine.

In our own day, the pervasive influence of leadership on the daily life of entire populations need no longer be imputed. For good or evil, it is openly proclaimed, centrally organized, and continuously growing. The development of corporate economies under centralized governments in the major countries of the world is such that we may say, without exaggeration, that never before have so few men affected so many different fields at once. The key decisions in politics, economies, foreign relations, military and naval affairs, education, housing, public works, and relief, and—save in Anglo-America—in religion, art, literature, music, architecture, and science are made by a handful of national leaders, and frequently by one figure whose judgment and taste become the absolute laws of the land. The tremendous development of means of communication, which makes it possible to transmit decisions with the speed of light to every nook and corner, ensures an effectiveness of control never known before.

A Caesar, a Cromwell, a Napoleon could and did issue decrees in many fields. But these fields, administratively and functionally, were not knotted together so tightly as they are today. They could not exact universal obedience to their decrees, or even suppress criticism. Some avenues of escape could never be closed. Some asylums of the spirit remained inaccessible to their law-enforcement agencies. The active presence of conflicting tendencies not only in politics but in religion and philosophy, during the reign of absolute rulers of the past, showed that they could not box culture within the confines of their dogmas and edicts. Their failure was not for want of trying.

How different is the picture in much of the world today! A Hitler, a Stalin, a Mussolini not only can and do issue decrees in every field, from military organization to abstract art and music; such dictators enforce them one hundred per cent. Their decisions affect not only the possibilities of earning a livelihood—something not unique to totalitarian countries—but all education of children and adults, and both the direction and content of their nations' literature, art, and philosophy. They cannot, of course, command geniuses to rise in the fields they control but they can utterly destroy all nonconforming genius and talent. Through schools on every level, since literacy is a weapon; through the radio, which no one can escape if it is loud enough; through the press and cinema, to which men naturally turn for information and relaxation —they carry their education to the very "subconscious" of their people.

Silence and anonymity are no longer safeguards. All asylums of the spirit have been destroyed. The counsel of prudent withdrawal and disinterested curiosity from afar that Montaigne offered to those who would escape the political storms of their time—a counsel echoed by Saint-Beuve a century ago—would today almost certainly arouse the suspicions of the secret police. This not only marks the distance which Europe has come from the absolutisms of yesterday; it is a sign that, except for the leader and his entourage, everyone has lost his private life without acquiring a public one.

In democratic countries like England and America— democratic because the leadership is still largely responsible to representative bodies, and subject to vigorous criticism by rank and file citizens—the area and power of executive authority have been enormously expanded. This is in part a consequence of the trend toward state capitalism in their economies; in part a consequence of the necessity of total defense in the struggle for survival against totalitarian aggression. But whatever the reason, the facts are unmistakable and are becoming plainer and plainer every day. With the possible exception of the field of foreign policy, the discretionary powers of the American President and the British Cabinet Ministers in the last few years surpass anything dreamed of by their democratic forebears.

Where so few can apparently decide so much, it is not surprising that interest in the historical significance of outstanding individuals should be strong. It does not require theoretical sophistication to realize that everyone has a practical stake of the most concrete kind in whatever leadership exists. Personal views and virtues in the political high command may spell public disaster or welfare. For once, at least, Mr. Everyman's moral appraisal of those in high places—if only he can keep it above the plane of village gossip—has historical relevance and justification.

The fundamental logic of the situation to which we shall often recur, that gives intelligent point to contemporary interest in our theme is this: Either the main line of historical action and social development is literally inescapable or it is not. If it is, any existing leadership is a completely subsidiary element in determining the main historical pattern of today and tomorrow. If it is not inescapable, the question almost asks itself: to what extent is the character of a given leadership causally and, since men are involved, morally responsible for our historical position and future? As we shall see, those who do speak of the inescapability of a specific historical future either belie their words by their actions as well as by other words, or else they compound their belief in an inescapable future with another one in the inescapability of a certain specific leadership, usually their own, which will lead us to this future. Sometimes they do both. We also shall see that to deny the inescapability of the main line of historical action does not *necessarily* mean that what it *will* be always depends upon the character of the leadership. There are more things in history than "laws of destiny" and "great men." As far as the historical role of leadership is concerned, it is a question of degree and types of situation. Our task will be to indicate roughly to what degrees and in what types of situation, it is legitimate to say that leadership does redetermine the historical trends by which it is confronted, and in what type of situations it is legitimate to say that it does not. . . .

Today, more than ever before, *belief* in "the hero" is a synthetic product. Whoever controls the microphones and printing presses can make or unmake belief overnight. If greatness be defined in terms of popular acclaim, as some hasty writers have suggested, then it may be thrust upon the modern dictator. But if it is not thrust upon him, he can easily arrange for it. It would, however, be a serious

error to assume that the individual who affects history—
that is, who helps redetermine the direction of historical
events—must get himself believed in or acclaimed, as a
condition of his historical effectiveness. Neither Peter the
Great nor Frederick II had a mass following. It is only
in modern times, where populations are literate, and lip
allegiance to the democratic ethos prevails even in countries where its political forms are flouted, that the leader
must get himself believed in to enhance his effectiveness.
It should also be noted that the modern leader or dictator
has emerged in a period of mass movements. In consequence he must have a mass base of support and belief
as a counterweight to other mass movements. Mass belief
in him before he reaches power is born of despair out of
need, and nurtured by unlimited promises. Once he takes
the reins, the dictator needs some mass support to consolidate his power. After that he can manufacture popular
belief in his divinely ordained or historically determined
mission almost at will.

Mass acclaim, which was not a necessary condition of
the leader's effectiveness in past eras, is not a sufficient
condition of historical effectiveness in the present. A fig-
urehead like the King of Italy or a royal romantic like
Edward VIII may be very popular, but he decides nothing.
For our purpose the apotheosis of an historical figure is
relevant only when it permits him to do historically
significant things which he would have been unable to
accomplish were he unpopular or without a mass following. . . .

Fashions of interpretation have shuttled back and forth
between historians and philosophers of history during the
last hundred years. On the one hand we have sweeping
forms of social determinism according to which the great
man is a symbol, an index, an expression, an instrument
or a consequence of historical laws. To be sure, distinguishing traits between a great man and other men are
recognized. But as a forceful writer of this school has put
it, "The 'distinguishing traits' of a person are merely individual scratches made by a higher law of [social] development." On the other hand, we have the conception of
the possibility of perpetual transformation of history by
innovators whose existence, strategic position, and shat-

tering effect upon their fellow men cannot ever be derived from the constellation of social forces of their day. Intermediate views have not been wanting. They have expressed little more than the eclectic belief that sometimes the great man and sometimes the weight of environment controls the direction of historical change. But they have not specified the general conditions under which these factors acquire determining significance. . . .

The social determinists usually have a more sober view of the specificity of talent and genius. For them social conditions are not always permissive to genius; they may be crushing. And when they are permissive, there are limits to the range of possibilities of heroic action. These limits can be inferred from the whole complex of social traditions, habits, tools and techniques, and the clash of group interests. It is this complex of culture traits which, without explaining the existence of genius, throws some light on its historical development and responsiveness to the "ripe" conditions. Carlyle would have held that Newton born into a community of Australian primitives would necessarily have made some major scientific discovery and that a Napoleon would have been a great savage military chieftain. Plechanov and other social determinists, on the other hand, realize that man is an "acculturated organism," to employ a favorite expression of John Dewey. He is dependent for his intellectual power not only upon his biological capacities but upon the society that sets the framework of interest and attention within which doubt and inquiry arise, and that supplies the very words which both inspire and limit the ideas that germinate within him. There is no good reason to believe that if a man with the biological endowment of Newton or Raphael or Napoleon had been born in early prehistory he would have rediscovered fire or created magnificent ornaments and paintings or achieved renown as a warrior.

The social determinists left a richer bequest to modern thought than an insight into the multiple ways in which genius is tied to culture. They made us sensitive to the *interrelatedness* of the different expressions of culture although they absurdly overstated the extent of the interrelation. But of greatest importance was their insistence on the notion of determining trends in history which, despite the mystical metaphysics that accompanied it, expressed a certain truth. . . .

It follows from what we have said that heroic action can count decisively only where the historical situation permits of major *alternative* paths of development. The denial by social determinists of the orthodox Marxist school that heroic action can ever have a decisive influence on history is usually a corollary to the doctrine that the existing mode of economic production *uniquely* determines the culture on which it is based. According to them, from a given economic system, one and only one other economic system can develop. And on the basis of the economic system thus developed, one and only one culture—where "culture" designates the noneconomic social institutions—can flourish. Where significant variations in the politics, art, religion, or philosophy are recognized, these must be explained "in the last analysis" in terms of the developmental changes of the economic system moved by its immanent "contradictions." Heroes in such a conception can be found only in the interstices and joints, so to speak, of the social economic process. Their presence is irrelevant to the death and birth of new forms of society. . . .

The existence of possible alternatives of development in a historic situation is the presupposition of significant heroic action. . . .

Where a genuine alternative exists, the active presence of a great man may be decisive—*may* be because *other* elements come into play to decide the issue between the alternatives, and they may weigh more heavily than the element of personality.

Wherever we are in a position to assert, as we shall assert below, that an event-making man has had a decisive influence on a historical period, we are not abandoning the belief in causal connection or embracing a belief in absolute contingency. What we are asserting is that in such situations the great man is a relatively independent historical influence—*independent of the conditions that determine the alternatives*—and that on these occasions the influence of all other relevant factors is of subordinate weight in enabling us to understand or predict which one of the possible alternatives will be actualized. In such

situations we also should be able to say, and to present
the grounds for saying, that if the great man had *not*
existed, the course of events in essential respects would
in all likelihood have taken a *different* turn. . . .

Our conclusion then is that without meeting some social
and group interests—economic, national, psychological—
the hero cannot influence historical events; but he meets
them in such a way that he always retains a considerable
degree of freedom in choosing which interests to further
and which to suppress or weaken. The behavior of most
historical figures in relation to political and social issues
can be explained in terms of the interests that speak
through them. But there are individuals in history who
not only talk back but react in such a way as to modify
the original relations of social interest in a radical way.

B. THE INDIVIDUAL AS LEADER

— 1 —

MEIN KAMPF
Adolf Hitler*

*The folkish philosophy is basically distinguished from
the Marxist philosophy by the fact that it not only recognizes the value of race, but with it the importance of the
personality, which it therefore makes one of the pillars
of its entire edifice.* These are the factors which sustain
its view of life.

If the National Socialist movement did not understand

* The selections from Adolf Hitler, *Mein Kampf* (Ralph
  Manheim, trans.), 1943, pp. 448-450, 509-510, 516-517,
  are reprinted by permission of and arrangement with
  Houghton Mifflin Company, the authorized publishers,
  and the Hutchinson Publishing Group.

the fundamental importance of this basic realization, but instead were merely to perform superficial patchwork on the present-day state, or even adopt the mass standpoint as its own—then it would really constitute nothing but a party in competition with the Marxists; in that case, it would not possess the right to call itself a philosophy of life. If the social program of the movement consisted only in pushing aside the personality and replacing it by the masses, National Socialism itself would be corroded by the poison of Marxism, as is the case with our bourgeois parties.

The folkish state must care for the welfare of its citizens by recognizing in all and everything the importance of the value of personality, thus in all fields preparing the way for that highest measure of productive performance which grants to the individual the highest measure of participation.

And accordingly, the folkish state must free all leadership and especially the highest—that is, the political leadership—entirely from the parliamentary principle of majority rule—in other words, mass rule—and instead absolutely guarantee the right of the personality.

From this the following realization results:

The best state constitution and state form is that which, with the most unquestioned certainty, raises the best minds in the national community to leading position and leading influence.

But as, in economic life, the able men cannot be appointed from above, but must struggle through for themselves, and just as here the endless schooling, ranging from the smallest business to the largest enterprise, occurs spontaneously, with life alone giving the examinations, obviously political minds cannot be 'discovered.' Extraordinary geniuses permit of no consideration for normal mankind.

From the smallest community cell to the highest leadership of the entire Reich, the state must have the personality principle anchored in its organization.

There must be no majority decisions, but only responsible persons, and the word 'council' must be restored to its original meaning. Surely every man will have advisers by his side, but *the decision will be made by one man.*

The principle which made the Prussian army in its time into the most wonderful instrument of the German people must someday, in a transferred sense, become the principle of the construction of our whole state conception: *authority of every leader downward and responsibility upward*.

Even then it will not be possible to dispense with those corporations which today we designate as parliaments. But their councillors will then actually give counsel; responsibility, however, can and may be borne only by *one* man, and therefore only he alone may possess the authority and right to command.

Parliaments as such are necessary, because in them, above all, personalities to which special responsible tasks can later be entrusted have an opportunity gradually to rise up.

This gives the following picture:

The folkish state, from the township up to the Reich leadership, has no representative body which decides anything by the majority, but only *advisory bodies* which stand at the side of the elected leader, receiving their share of work from him, and in turn if necessary assuming unlimited responsibility in certain fields, just as on a larger scale the leader or chairman of the various corporations himself possesses. . . .

The tragic reason why in the solution of a single task we usually do not content ourselves with a single association is the following: Every deed in the grand manner on this earth will in general be the fulfillment of a desire which had long since been present in millions of people, a longing silently harbored by many. Yes, it can come about that centuries wish and yearn for the solution of a certain question, because they are sighing beneath the intolerable burden of an existing condition and the fulfillment of this general longing does not materialize. Nations which no longer find any heroic solution for such distress can be designated as *impotent*, while we see the vitality of a people, and the predestination for life guaranteed by this vitality, most strikingly demonstrated when, for a people's liberation from a great oppression, or for the elimination of a bitter distress, or for the satisfaction of its soul, restless because it has grown insecure—Fate some day bestows upon it the man endowed for this purpose, who finally brings the long yearned-for fulfillment.

Now it lies entirely in the essence of so-called great questions of the day that thousands are active in their solution, that many feel called, indeed, that Fate itself puts forward many for selection, and then ultimately, in the free play of forces, gives victory to the stronger and more competent, entrusting him with the solution of the problem. . . .

It must never be forgotten that nothing that is really great in this world has ever been achieved by coalitions; but that it has always been the success of a single victor. Coalition successes bear by the very nature of their origin the germ of future crumbling, in fact of the loss of what has already been achieved. Great, truly world-shaking revolutions of a spiritual nature are not even conceivable and realizable except as the titanic struggles of individual formations, never as enterprises of coalitions.

And thus the folkish state above all will never be created by the compromising will of a folkish working federation, but solely by the iron will of a single movement that has fought its way to the top against all.

— 2 —

ESSAYS IN SOCIOLOGY
Max Weber*

Bureaucratic and patriarchal structures are antagonistic in many ways, yet they have in common a most im-

* *From Max Weber: Essays in Sociology,* translated and edited by H. H. Gerth and C. Wright Mills. Copyright 1946 by Oxford University Press, Inc., pp. 245-262. Reprinted by permission.

portant peculiarity: permanence. In this respect they are both institutions of daily routine. Patriarchal power especially is rooted in the provisioning of recurrent and normal needs of the workaday life. Patriarchal authority thus has its original locus in the economy, that is, in those branches of the economy that can be satisfied by means of normal routine. The patriarch is the 'natural leader' of the daily routine. And in this respect, the bureaucratic structure is only the counter-image of patriarchalism transposed into rationality. As a permanent structure with a system of rational rules, bureaucracy is fashioned to meet calculable and recurrent needs by means of a normal routine.

The provisioning of all demands that go beyond those of everyday routine has had, in principle, an entirely heterogeneous, namely, a *charismatic,* foundation; the further back we look in history, the more we find this to be the case. This means that the 'natural' leaders—in times of psychic, physical, economic, ethical, religious, political distress—have been neither officeholders nor incumbents of an 'occupation' in the present sense of the word, that is, men who have acquired expert knowledge and who serve for remuneration. The natural leaders in distress have been holders of specific gifts of the body and spirit; and these gifts have been believed to be supernatural, not accessible to everybody. The concept of 'charisma' is here used in a completely 'value-neutral' sense. . . .

In contrast to any kind of bureaucratic organization of offices, the charismatic structure knows nothing of a form or of an ordered procedure of appointment or dismissal. It knows no regulated 'career,' 'advancement,' 'salary,' or regulated and expert training of the holder of charisma or of his aids. It knows no agency of control or appeal, no local bailiwicks or exclusive functional jurisdictions; nor does it embrace permanent institutions like our bureaucratic 'departments,' which are independent of persons and of purely personal charisma.

Charisma knows only inner determination and inner restraint. The holder of charisma seizes the task that is adequate for him and demands obedience and a following by virtue of his mission. His success determines whether he finds them. His charismatic claim breaks down if his mission is not recognized by those to whom he feels he has been sent. If they recognize him, he is their master—so long as he knows how to maintain recognition through 'proving' himself. But he does not derive his 'right' from their will, in the manner of an election. Rather, the reverse holds: it is the *duty* of those to whom he addresses his mission to recognize him as their charismatically qualified leader. . . .

In order to do justice to their mission, the holders of charisma, the master as well as his disciples and followers, must stand outside the ties of this world, outside of routine occupations, as well as outside the routine obligations of family life. . . .

By its very nature, the existence of charismatic authority is specifically unstable. The holder may forego his charisma; he may feel 'forsaken by his God,' as Jesus did on the cross; he may prove to his followers that 'virtue is gone out of him.' It is then that his mission is extinguished, and hope waits and searches for a new holder of charisma. The charismatic holder is deserted by his following, however, (only) because pure charisma does not know any 'legitimacy' other than that flowing from personal strength, that is, one which is constantly being proved. The charismatic hero does not deduce his authority from codes and statutes, as is the case with the jurisdiction of office; nor does he deduce his authority from traditional custom or feudal vows of faith, as is the case with patrimonial power.

The charismatic leader gains and maintains authority solely by proving his strength in life. If he wants to be a prophet, he must perform miracles; if he wants to be a war lord, he must perform heroic deeds. Above all, however, his divine mission must 'prove' itself in that those who faithfully surrender to him must fare well. If they do not fare well, he is obviously not the master sent by the gods.

This very serious meaning of genuine charisma evidently stands in radical contrast to the convenient pretensions of present rulers to a 'divine right of kings,' with its reference to the 'inscrutable' will of the Lord, 'to whom alone the monarch is responsible.' The genuinely charismatic ruler is responsible precisely to those whom he rules. He is responsible for but one thing, that he personally and actually be the God-willed master.

During these last decades we have witnessed how the Chinese monarch impeaches himself before all the people because of his sins and insufficiencies if his administration does not succeed in warding off some distress from the governed, whether it is inundations or unsuccessful wars. Thus does a ruler whose power, even in vestiges and theoretically, is genuinely charismatic deport himself. And if even this penitence does not reconcile the deities, the charismatic emperor faces dispossession and death, which often enough is consummated as a propitiatory sacrifice.

Meng-tse's (Mencius') thesis that the people's voice is 'God's voice' (according to him the *only* way in which God speaks!) has a very specific meaning: if the people cease to recognize the ruler, it is expressly stated that he simply becomes a private citizen; and if he then wishes to be more, he becomes a usurper deserving of punishment. The state of affairs that corresponds to these phrases, which sound highly revolutionary, recurs under primitive conditions without any such pathos. The charismatic character adheres to almost all primitive authorities with the exception of domestic power in the narrowest sense, and the chieftain is often enough simply deserted if success does not remain faithful to him.

The subjects may extend a more active or passive 'recognition' to the personal mission of the charismatic master. His power rests upon this purely factual recognition and springs from faithful devotion. It is devotion to the extraordinary and unheard-of, to what is strange to all rule and tradition and which therefore is viewed as divine. It is a devotion born of distress and enthusiasm.

Genuine charismatic domination therefore knows of no abstract legal codes and statutes and of no 'formal' way of adjudication. Its 'objective' law emanates concretely from the highly personal experience of heavenly grace and from the god-like strength of the hero. Charismatic domination means a rejection of all ties to any external order in favor of the exclusive glorification of the genuine mentality of the prophet and hero. Hence, its attitude is revolutionary and transvalues everything; it makes a sovereign break with all traditional or rational norms: 'It is written, but I say unto you.' . . .

It is the fate of charisma, whenever it comes into the permanent institutions of a community, to give way to powers of tradition or of rational socialization. This waning of charisma generally indicates the diminishing importance of individual action. And of all those powers that lessen the importance of individual action, the most irresistible is *rational discipline*. . . .

Charisma, as a creative power, recedes in the face of domination, which hardens into lasting institutions, and becomes efficacious only in short-lived mass emotions of incalculable effects, as on elections and similar occasions. Nevertheless charisma remains a highly important element of the social structure, although of course in a greatly changed sense.

We must now return to the economic factors, already mentioned above, which predominantly determine the routinization of charisma: the need of social strata, privileged through existing political, social, and economic orders, to have their social and economic positions 'legitimized.' They wish to see their positions transformed from purely factual power relations into a cosmos of acquired rights, and to know that they are thus sanctified. These interests comprise by far the strongest motive for the conservation of charismatic elements of an objectified nature within the structure of domination. Genuine charisma is absolutely opposed to this objectified form. It does not appeal to an enacted or traditional order, nor does it base its claims upon acquired rights. Genuine charisma rests upon the legitimation of personal heroism or personal revelation. Yet precisely this quality of charisma as an extraordinary, supernatural, divine power transforms it, after its routinization, into a suitable source for the legitimate acquisition of sovereign power by the successors of the charismatic hero. Routinized charisma thus continues to work in favor of all those whose power and possession is guaranteed by that sovereign power, and who thus depend upon the continued existence of such power.

C. THE PARTY AS LEADER

— 1 —

WHAT IS TO BE DONE?
V. I. Lenin*

The time has come when Russian revolutionists, led by a genuine revolutionary theory, relying upon the genuinely revolutionary and spontaneously awakening class, can at last—at last!—rise to their full height and exert their giant strength to the utmost. All that is required in order that this may be so is that the masses of our practical workers and the still larger masses of those who dream of doing practical work even while still at school shall meet with scorn and ridicule any suggestion that may be made to degrade our political tasks, and to restrict the scope of our organizational work. . . .

Such workers, average people of the masses, are capable of displaying enormous energy and self-sacrifice in strikes and in street battles, with the police and troops, and are capable (in fact, are alone capable) of *determining* the whole outcome of our movement—but the struggle against the *political* police requires special qualities; it can be conducted only by *professional* revolutionists. And we must not only see to it that the masses "advance" concrete demands, but also that the masses of the workers "advance" an increasing number of such professional revolutionists from their own ranks. Thus we have reached the question of the relation between an organization of professional revolutionists and the pure and simple labour movement. . . .

* V. I. Lenin, *What Is To Be Done?*, International Publishers, 1929, pp. 101-104, 112-116, 124-131.

Secret strikes are impossible—for those who take a direct and immediate part in them, but a strike may remain (and in the majority of cases does remain) a "secret" to the masses of the Russian workers, because the government takes care to cut all communication between strikers, takes care to prevent all news of strikes from spreading. Now here indeed is a special "struggle against the political police" required, a struggle that can never be conducted by such large masses as usually take part in strikes. Such a struggle must be organized, according to "all the rules of the art," by people who are professionally engaged in revolutionary activity. The fact that the masses are spontaneously entering the movement does not make the organization of this struggle *less necessary*. On the contrary, it makes it *more necessary;* for we Socialists would be failing in our duty to the masses if we did not prevent the police from making a secret of (and if we did not ourselves sometimes secretly prepare) every strike and every demonstration. *And we will succeed in doing this,* precisely because the spontaneously awakening masses will *also advance from their own ranks* increasing numbers of "professional revolutionists" (that is, if we are not so foolish as to advise the workers to keep on marking time). . . .

A small compact core, consisting of reliable, experienced, and hardened workers, with responsible agents in the principal districts and connected by all the rules of strict secrecy with the organizations of revolutionists, can, with the wide support of the masses and without an elaborate set of rules, perform *all* the functions of a trade-union organization, and perform them, moreover, in the manner Social-Democrats desire. Only in this way can we secure the *consolidation* and development of a *Social-Democratic* trade-union movement, in spite of the gendarmes.

It may be objected that an organization which is so loose that it is not even formulated, and which even has no enrolled and registered members, cannot be called an organization at all. That may very well be. I am not out for names. But this "organization without members" can do everything that is required, and will, from the very outset, guarantee the closest contact between our future trade unionists and Socialism. Only an incorrigible utopian would want a *wide* organization of workers, with elections, reports, universal suffrage, etc., under autocracy.

The moral to be drawn from this is a simple one. If we begin with the solid foundation of a strong organization of revolutionists, we can guarantee the stability of the movement as a whole, and carry out the aims of both Social-Democracy and of trade unionism. If, however, we begin with a wide workers' organization, supposed to be most "accessible" to the masses, when as a matter of fact it will be most accessible to the gendarmes, and will make the revolutionists most accessible to the police, we shall neither achieve the aims of Social-Democracy nor of trade unionism. . . .

"A dozen wise men can be more easily caught than a hundred fools!" This wonderful truth (which the hundred fools will applaud) appears obvious only because in the very midst of the argument you have skipped from one question to another. You began by talking, and continued to talk, of catching a "committee," of catching an "organization," and now you skip to the question of getting hold of the "roots" of the movement in the "depths." The fact is, of course, that our movement cannot be caught precisely because it has hundreds and hundreds of thousands of roots deep down among the masses, but that is not the point we are discussing. As far as "roots in the depths" are concerned, we cannot be "caught" even now, in spite of all our primitiveness; but, we all complain, and cannot but complain, of the ease with which the *organizations* can be caught, with the result that it is impossible to maintain continuity in the movement. If you agree to discuss the question of catching the *organizations,* and to stick to that question, then I assert that it is far more difficult to catch ten wise men than it is to catch a hundred fools. And this premise I shall defend no matter how much you instigate the crowd against me for my "anti-democratic" views, etc. As I have already said, by "wise men," in connection with organization, I mean *professional revolutionists,* irrespective of whether they are students or working men. I assert:

1. That no movement can be durable without a stable organization of leaders to maintain continuity;

2. That the more widely the masses are drawn into the struggle and form the basis of the movement, the more necessary is it to have such an organisation and the more stable must it be (for it is much easier then for demagogues to side-track the more backward sections of the masses);

3. That the organisation must consist chiefly of persons engaged in revolution as a profession;

4. That in a country with a despotic government, the more we *restrict* the membership of this organisation to persons who are engaged in revolution as a profession and who have been professionally trained in the art of combating the political police, the more difficult will it be to catch the organisation; and

5. The *wider* will be the circle of men and women of the working class or of other classes of society able to join the movement and perform active work in it. . . .

As the spontaneous rise of the labouring masses becomes wider and deeper, it not only promotes from its ranks an increasing number of talented agitators, but also of talented organisers, propagandists, and "practical workers" in the best sense of the term (of whom there are so few among our intelligentsia). In the majority of cases, the latter are somewhat careless and sluggish in their habits (so characteristic of Russians). When we shall have detachments of specially trained working-class revolutionists who have gone through long years of preparation (and, of course, revolutionists "of all arms") no political police in the world will be able to contend against them, for these detachments will consist of men absolutely devoted and loyal to the revolution, and will themselves enjoy the absolute confidence and devotion of the broad masses of the workers. The *sin* we commit is that we do not sufficiently "stimulate" the workers to take this path, "common" to them and to the "intellectuals," of professional revolutionary training, and that we too frequently drag them back by our silly speeches about what "can be understood" by the masses of the workers, by the "average workers," etc. . . .

It is further argued against us that the views on organisation here expounded contradict the "principles of democracy." . . .

Every one will probably agree that "broad principles of democracy" presupposes the two following conditions: first, full publicity and second, election to all functions. It would be absurd to speak about democracy without publicity, that is a publicity that extends beyond the circle of the membership of the organisation. We call the German Socialist Party a democratic organization because all it does is done publicly; even its party congresses are held in public. But no one would call an organisation that is hidden from everyone but its members by a veil of secrecy, a democratic organisation. What is the use of advancing "*broad* principles of democracy" when the fundamental condition for this principle *cannot be fulfilled* by a secret organisation. "Broad principles" turns out to be a resonant, but hollow phrase. More than that, this phrase proves that the urgent tasks in regard to organisation are totally misunderstood. Every one knows how great is the lack of secrecy among the "broad" masses of revolutionists. . . .

Nor is the situation with regard to the second attribute of democracy, namely, the principle of election, any better. In politically free countries, this condition is taken for granted. "Membership of the party is open to those who accept the principles of the party programme, and render all the support they can to the party"—says paragraph 1 of the rules of the German Social-Democratic Party. And as the political arena is as open to the public view as is the stage in a theatre, this acceptance or non-acceptance, support or opposition is announced to all in the press and at public meetings. Every one knows that a certain political worker commenced in a certain way, passed through a certain evolution, behaved in difficult periods in a certain way; every one knows all his qualities, and consequently, knowing all the facts of the case, *every party member can decide for himself whether or not to elect this person for a certain party office*. The general control (in the literal sense of the term) that the party exercises over every act this person commits on the political field brings into being an automatically operating mechanism which brings about what in biology is called "survival of the fittest." "Natural selection," full publicity, the principle of election and general control provide the guarantee that, in the last analysis, every political worker will be "in his proper place," will do the work for which he is best fitted, will feel the effects of his mistakes on himself, and prove before all the world his ability to recognise mistakes and to avoid them.

Try to put this picture in the frame of our autocracy! Is it possible in Russia for all those "who accept the principles of the party programme and render it all the support they can," to control every action of the revolutionist working in secret? Is it possible for all the revolutionists to elect one of their number to any particular office when, in the very interests of the work, *he must conceal his identity* from nine out of ten of these "all"? Ponder a little over the real meaning of the high-sounding phrases that *Rabocheye Dyelo* gives utterance to, and you will realise that "broad democracy" in party organization, amidst the gloom of autocracy and the domination of the gendarmes, is nothing more than a *useless and harmful toy*. It is a useless toy, because as a matter of fact, no revolutionary organization has ever practiced *broad* democracy, nor could it, however much it desired to do so. It is a harmful toy, because any attempt to practice the "broad principles of democracy" will simply facilitate the work of the police in making big raids, it will perpetuate the prevailing primitiveness, divert the thoughts of the practical workers from the serious and imperative task of training themselves to become professional revolutionists to that of drawing up detailed "paper" rules for election systems. Only abroad, where very often people who have no opportunity of doing real live work gather together, can the "game of democracy" be played here and there, especially in small groups. . . .

The only serious organisational principle the active workers of our movement can accept is: Strict secrecy, strict selection of members, and the training of professional revolutionists. If we possessed these qualities, "democracy" and something even more would be guaranteed to us, namely: Complete, comradely, mutual confidence among revolutionists. And this something more

is absolutely essential for us because, in Russia, it is useless to think that democratic control can serve as a
substitute for it. It would be a great mistake to believe
that because it is impossible to establish real "democratic" control, the members of the revolutionary organisation will remain altogether uncontrolled. They have
not the time to think about the toy forms of democracy
(democracy within a close and compact body enjoying
the complete mutual confidence of the comrades), but
they have a lively sense of their *responsibility*, because
they know from experience that an organization of real
revolutionsts will stop at nothing to rid itself of an undesirable member. Moreover, there is a very well-devel-
oped public opinion in Russian (and international) revolutionary circles which has a long history behind it, and
which sternly and ruthlessly punishes every departure
from the duties of comradeship (and does not "democracy," real and not toy democracy, represent a part of
the conception of comradeship?). Take all this into consideration and you will realize that all the talk and resolutions that come from abroad about "anti-democratic
tendencies" has a nasty odour of the playing at generals
that goes on there.

— 2 —

HOW TO BE A COMMUNIST PARTY MEMBER (1939)

Ch'en Yün*

According to the policy of Lenin, only those who actually participate in the organization, unreservedly obey

* Reprinted by permission of the publishers from Conrad
   Brandt, Benjamin Schwartz and John K. Fairbank, *A*

the organization and are willing to devote themselves heart, body, and soul to the mission of the Party of Communism may become CP members. Lenin fought against Martov in order to establish his principles of Party organization, resolutely opposing Martov's proposal that persons be admitted to Party membership without actual participation or even the intention to participate but merely by giving sympathy or support outside the (Party) organization. This 100 per cent opportunist viewpoint not only obliterates the distinction between Party and class, but also changes the nature of the Party, degrading it to (the status of) a labour union or students' federation, making the Party "sink into a sea of sympathizers and opens the door for unstable, wavering, and opportunist elements" (Lenin). Thus the participation in a specific organization of the Party and positive work for the Party are the minimum requirements for each Party member. . . .

Workers are the foundation of the Party, and the Party must pay particular attention to the strengthening of the worker elements in our organization. Nevertheless, the Party will not refuse to admit people of other class origins who have undergone the training of daily economic struggle and of the revolutionary movement. They must, however, give up their former unproletarian, anti-Communist viewpoint and subscribe to the programme and Constitution of the Party before they can be admitted to the Party. Accordingly, the Party is firmly opposed to any viewpoint that does not insist on the purity of Party composition or the strengthening of its proletarian core, thus degrading the Party to a "national revolutionary alliance" of all classes. . . .

For a new member to be admitted to the Party he must be sponsored by a (Party) member or members in accordance with Party provisions and current rules: for workers and hired farm hands, one sponsor; for a petty bourgeois, two sponsors; for those who leave other political parties to join our Party, three sponsors—approved by a Party group and *chih-pu* (Party cell) and certified

Documentary History of Chinese Communism, Harvard University Press and George Allen and Unwin, Ltd., 1952, pp. 322-323, 326, 327, 330-333.

by a higher Party committee. Those who have once belonged to other political groups must be approved by the district Party committee, the Central Branch Bureau, or the CC (of the CCP) (before they can be admitted into the Party).

The CP is a party fighting for the complete liberation of mankind as well as for Communism and its proletarian mission. Therefore a CP member who is willing to dedicate himself to the Communist cause must not only fight for Communism, but also formulate a revolutionary view of life which will lead him to fight relentlessly for the realization of Communism. But how can one formulate and consolidate one's view of life? First of all, it is necessary to understand the pattern of historic development of human society and have a firm faith in the inevitable realization of a Communist society in the future. That is to say, a CP member should, on the basis of his class consciousness, his practical revolutionary experience, and his understanding of Marxism, grasp thoroughly the historic position and role of the proletariat in society, comprehend the interests of the proletariat and its liberating mission, and clearly discern the immediate policies and goal of the CP and its members. Only thus can he firmly formulate his view of life, follow it throughout his life, and struggle to the end for the realization of his convictions. At the same time, every member of the CCP should thoroughly understand that the Chinese revolution is a long, hazardous task, and that on the winding, treacherous path of revolution, a revolutionary must be prepared for prolonged hardship and set-backs; he must also be prepared at a critical moment to sacrifice his very life. Therefore, every CP member should not only have an unwavering faith in the realization of Communism, but also be resolved to fight to the very end, undaunted by either sacrifices or hardships, for the liberation of the working class, the Chinese nation, and the Chinese people.

Our Party is a political party aiming at the complete liberation of the proletariat of China, the entire Chinese nation and people, and the establishment of a Communist society; thus, the interests of the nation and the people and those of the Party are identical. CP members are fighters for a Communist mission under the leadership of the Party. Thus the interests of a Party member are identical with those of the nation, the people, and the Party. Every Party member should give his unlimited devotion to the nation, to the revolution, to our class, and to the Party, subordinating individual interests to those of the nation, the revolution, our class, and the Party.

However, in the course of revolutionary work as well as Party work, the individual interests of Party members may come into conflict with those of the Party. At such a time, every Party member should fall back on his unlimited devotion to the revolution and the Party, sacrifice unhesitatingly his individual interests and bow to the over-all interests of the revolution and the Party. (He must) put the interests of the revolution and the Party in the first place and deal with all individual issues on the principle that revolutionary and Party interests stand above all others. He must not place individual interests above those of the revolution and the Party.

"The interests of the revolution and Party above ALL" is not an empty phrase. The Party not only demands that Party members understand this phrase, but also emphatically calls on every Party member to carry out this motto resolutely and unhesitatingly in practical life and in every concrete act of daily life. Only when our Party has members who are willing to sacrifice everything for the interests of the revolution and the Party can the successful accomplishment of the revolution by the Party be assured. . . .

Therefore, it is the duty of every CP member to observe Party discipline resolutely and conscientiously. He should not only struggle with the tendencies that tend to undermine Party discipline, but should also struggle hard with his own words and actions which may tend to endanger Party discipline, in order to become a model in observing Party discipline. Do not think that merely stating one's support of, and voting for, the Party line at meetings or in the presence of the masses are enough for observing Party discipline; it is far from adequate. A good Party member who truly and conscientiously maintains discipline proves this discipline by his actions and dealings in the concrete issues of daily life. He shows himself to be a model in his resolute observation of the iron discipline of the Party. . . .

It is not enough for a CP member to support the resolutions of the Party verbally; it is his duty to carry out those resolutions with determination and put these resolutions into practice in his actions. In carrying out Party resolutions, it is sometimes inevitable that certain difficulties and set-backs may be encountered. CP members must overcome such handicaps with an unflinching and unbending spirit. Performing Party work passively like an indifferent employee is absolutely impermissible. The Chinese revolution is a task that involves tedious, prolonged struggles. One of the characteristics of the CCP is its indomitable spirit of sacrifice and struggle. Every CCP member must possess this hard-fighting spirit if he is to inherit and glorify the splendid tradition of the Party.

— 3 —

ON THE INTRA-PARTY STRUGGLE (1941)
Liu Shao-ch'i*

Comrades! Recently we have raised in the Party the problem of strengthening the Party spirit among Party members. I have heard that the CC has passed a resolution on this question and that we shall be able to obtain it before long. In order to strengthen the Party spirit among Party members, we have to develop a series of

* Reprinted by permission of the publishers from Conrad Brandt, Benjamin Schwartz and John K. Fairbank, *A Documentary History of Chinese Communism*, Harvard University Press and George Allen and Unwin, Ltd., 1952, pp. 356-358, 366-368, 371-372.

concrete struggles in thought so that all types of undesirable tendencies transgressing that spirit will be opposed. But what is to be considered the correct method of developing the struggles in thought within the Party and what is to be considered the incorrect method? This is the question I would now like to discuss. . . .

Everyone knows that our Party is a party of the proletariat, that it leads the broad masses to battle. . . . The Party and the proletariat have been constantly encircled by the power of the non-proletarian classes: the big and petty bourgeoisie, the peasantry, and even the remnants of feudal forces. These classes, either struggling against the proletariat or in alliance with it, have infiltrated, through the unstable elements within the Party and proletariat, to their heart, and constantly influenced them in ideology, living habits, theory, and action. This, then, is the source of all erroneous, evil tendencies within the Party. It is the social origin of all opportunism within the Party and also the source of the intra-Party struggle.

The intra-Party struggle is a reflection of the struggle outside the Party.

Since the day of its origin the Party has not only fought enemies outside the Party, but has also fought the non-proletarian influences of enemies within the Party. The two struggles are to be distinguished, but both are necessary and, in class substance, they are the same. If the Party does not engage in the second struggle, if it does not constantly carry out a struggle to oppose all undesirable tendencies within the Party, does not constantly reject all non-proletarian ideology and overcome "left" and right opportunism, then non-proletarian ideology and "left" and right opportunism will be able to develop in the Party and influence and guide the Party. . . .

This intra-Party struggle is primarily the struggle in thought, the contents of which are divergencies and mutual opposition in principles of thought. In the Party, even though divergencies and mutual opposition among the comrades can lead to political divergencies and even, under certain conditions, unavoidably lead to divergencies concerning Party organization, the struggle in thought remains its basic substance and content. Therefore an intra-Party struggle which does not contain divergencies in principles of thought, but only embodies personal attacks among the comrades without principle, is a struggle without principle and without content. Within the Party this type of struggle—without principle and without content—is entirely unnecessary. It harms the Party and should be carefully avoided by Party members.

Intra-Party struggle is absolutely necessary to maintain the Party's purity and independence, to guarantee that Party activities are carried on the line which represents the highest interests of the proletariat, and to maintain the Party's proletarian substance. With this aim, the intra-Party struggle must proceed in two directions, advance on two fronts. (This is) because enemy thought influences the Party from two directions, because it attacks the Party from the right and from the "left," because it is manifested in the Party as right and "left" opportunism. Therefore, (in) the intra-Party struggle, (we) must oppose right opportunism. We must struggle against both, and only then will we be able to maintain the proletarian substance of our Party. . . .

Comrades! I am now going to speak on another deviation in the intra-Party struggle—the unprincipled struggle within the Party. The prevalence of this phenomenon is especially common and grave within the CCP. Although the so-called "gossip movement" exists in foreign Communist Parties, I think it probably is not so serious abroad as in the CCP. . . .

What are the unprincipled disputes and struggles in the Party?

I consider the following instances of dispute and struggle within the Party to be without principle; that is, they run counter to those common stands and principles which promote the interests of our Party and the proletarian revolution.

First: Some comrades do not raise questions and struggle with other comrades from a Party standpoint or for the sake of the interests of the entire Party, but do so from the standpoint of individual or fractional interests. This is to say, the stand from which they engage in the intra-Party struggle is incorrect. As a consequence, their views on problems and their solutions and methods in dealing with them are also incorrect. Only if their individual or minority interests are benefited do they give approval or support in dealing with a matter. If their individual or minority interests are not benefited, they stand in opposition and do not give their approval. They are unconcerned with the interests of the Party or the revolution and put these in a place of secondary importance. . . .

Second: Some comrades provoke conflicts and disputes within the Party, not to improve the Party, but with the opposite purpose in mind or other motives. This purpose is incorrect and the struggle they provoke is also without principle. For example, some comrades foment disputes in the Party and struggle with their comrades to show off, improve their position, save face, or even to vent their hatred and seek revenge. They upset their comrades' work and plans and wreck the order and solidarity of the Party, but fail to give their attention to prevailing circumstances and conditions. Such are the characteristics of this form of unprincipled struggle.

Third: Some comrades do not start from a basis of principle in raising questions for acceptance or rejection by the Party. It is only on the basis of their own feelings, likes and dislikes, that they raise questions and struggle, only for the emotional release of the moment or for the soothing of their ruffled tempers, that they revile others and give vent to their anger. This is also a form of struggle without principle. Some comrades, because their experience is limited or their theoretical level low, cannot raise questions for debate on the basis of principle. It is only on particular or miscellaneous questions, questions of a purely practical nature, or everyday administrative questions, which do not involve principle, that they debate with absolute obstinacy. But since this does not involve general questions of principle it is also an unprincipled form of struggle which should not be insisted on. . . .

The *fourth* (instance) is to engage in the intra-Party struggle unscrupulously or without observing organizational procedures, to befriend or attack comrades in an unprincipled way, provoking dissension, betraying or secretly scheming against comrades, or not speaking to a man's face, but speaking wildly behind his back, irresponsibly criticizing the Party, spreading unfounded opinions, circulating rumours, telling lies, and calumniating others.

The cases cited above are all examples of the struggle without principle. Next, there are also some comrades who infuse certain elements of unprincipled struggle into the struggle concerning principles, or who, under the protective banner of a struggle concerning principles, engage in a struggle which is without principle. In addition, there are some comrades who pay special attention to the quarrels between certain persons, or to the discordant relations between certain persons, instead of the substance of their controversy.

What are the origins of the unprincipled and the mechanical and excessive struggle within the Party? They spring from the following sources:

First: The generally low theoretical level of comrades in the Party and, in many respects, the insufficiency of their experience. For a long time, a leadership and "centre" for the entire Party have actually not materialized and the leadership and the "centre" in the various localities have, up to the present, materialized to only a very slight degree.

Second: The petty-bourgeois elements within the Party are strong and the rashness and madness of the petty-bourgeois, and the peasant petty-bourgeois spirit of revenge have constantly influenced the intra-Party struggle.

Third: The democratic life within the Party is not normal, a spirit of objective, mutual discussion of problems among the comrades has not developed, and the tendency to judge and decide problems in a crude, subjective manner is still prevalent to a serious degree.

Fourth: Opportunist elements have infiltrated into the Party, and a certain opportunist psychology exists in a group of comrades within the Party. In order to prove their own "bolshevization" they often intentionally go a little to the "left," thinking that "left" is better than right, or they attack others in order to raise their own prestige.

Fifth: Trotskyite spies and counter-revolutionary elements have infiltrated the Party, making use of the intra-Party struggle to sabotage the Party. Under the cover of the Party banner, traitorous Trotskyite elements often deliberately attack certain comrades, and after the attack still other traitorous Trotskyite elements absorb the comrades who thus have been attacked into the Trotskyite group as traitors. . . .

In brief, the intra-Party struggle consists basically of divergencies and struggle in thought and principle. All in the Party should reason, clear up the issues, and have some line of reasoning to speak about. Otherwise it is wrong. If lines of reasoning are thrashed out, there is nothing which cannot be done well and easily. In the Party, we should cultivate the spirit of reasoning. The standards by which to judge the correctness or incorrectness of a line of reasoning are the interest of the struggle being carried on by the Party and the proletariat, the submission of the partial interest to the interest of the whole, and the submission of the short-range interest to the long-range interest. All reasoning and all proposals which are in the interest of the struggle of the Party and proletariat—in the long-range interest of the struggle of the entire Party and proletariat—are correct. Those which are detrimental to these interests are all incorrect.

D. THE ARMY AS LEADER

— 1 —

ARMIES IN THE PROCESS OF POLITICAL MODERNIZATION
Lucian W. Pye*

The trend of recent years toward increased authoritarian rule and army-dominated governments raises ques-

* Reprinted from Lucian W. Pye, "Armies in the Process of Political Modernization," *The Role of the Military in*

tions which seem only to emphasize the limitations of our knowledge. Is it true, as we have always supposed, that any encroachment of the military into civilian rule is a blow to liberal government and civil liberties? Or is it possible that military rule can, in fact, establish the necessary basis for the growth of effective representative institutions? Have events reached such a state in parts of Asia that we should welcome army rule as the least odious of possible developments and probably the only effective counterforce to communism? We seem to be confronted by two conflicting images of the politician in uniform. The first, derived largely from Latin America and the Balkans, is that of administrative incompetence, inaction, and authoritarian, if not reactionary, values. The second and more recent is that of a dynamic and self-sacrificing military leadership committed to progress and the task of modernizing transitional societies that have been subverted by the "corrupt practices" of politicians. How is it possible to tell in any particular case whether army rule will lead to sterile authoritarianism or to vigorous development? . . .

The fact that these new armies in preindustrial societies are modeled after industrial-based organizations has many implications for their political roles. One of their characteristics is particularly significant: the specialization that modern armies demand in skills and functions is only distantly related to the command of violence. There has generally been a tremendous increase in the number of officers assigned to staff functions as contrasted with line commands. As the armies have striven to approximate their ideal models they have had to establish all manner of specialized organizations and departments that require skills that are either in short supply or nonexistent in their societies. The Burmese Army, for example, in addition to its engineer and signal corps has special sections on chemical warfare, psychological warfare, and even a historical and archaeological section. All the new armies have attempted to introduce specialized training schools and advanced techniques of per-

Underdeveloped Countries, John J. Johnson, ed., pp. 69-70, 76-78, by permission of Princeton University Press. Copyright © 1962 by the RAND Corporation.

sonnel management and procurement. Consequently, numbers of the more intelligent and ambitious officers have had to be trained in industrial skills more advanced than those common to the civilian economy.

The high proportion of officers assigned to staff functions means that large numbers of officers are forced to look outside their society for their models. The fact that army leaders, particularly the younger and more ambitious, generally come from those trained in staff positions means that they are extremely sensitive to the needs of modernization and technological advancement. This kind of sensitivity bears little relationship to the command of physical violence and tests of human endurance—in short, to the martial spirit as we customarily think of it. In consequence the officers often find that they are spiritually in tune with the intellectuals, students, and those other elements in society most anxious to become a part of the modern world. They may have little in common with the vast majority of the men they must command. In this respect the gap between the officer class and the troops, once largely a matter of social and economic class (as it still is to some degree), has now been widened by differences in the degree of acculturation to modern life.

It should be noted that these revolutionary changes in military life have significantly influenced the status of the military profession in different societies and hence have had an interesting effect on relative national power. Cultures that looked down on the military at an earlier stage of technology now accord high prestige to the same profession as it has raised its technology. For example, when armies depended entirely on human energy and animal power the Chinese placed the soldier near the bottom of the social hierarchy; with present levels of advanced military technology the soldier is now near the top of the social scale in both Communist and non-Communist China. The change has been more in the nature of the military profession than in basic Chinese cultural values. Conversely, peoples once considered "martial" may now show little interest in, or aptitude for, the new kind of soldiering.

Above all else, however, the revolution in military

technology has caused the army leaders of the newly emergent countries to be extremely sensitive to the extent to which their countries are economically and technologically underdeveloped. Called upon to perform roles basic to advanced societies, the more politically conscious officers can hardly avoid being aware of the need for substantial changes in their own societies.

— 2 —

MILITARISM AND POLITICS IN LATIN AMERICA
Edwin Lieuwen*

The recent decades of rapid change and social crisis in Latin America brought the armed forces back into a position of political prominence they had not held since the nineteenth century. At the time of World War I, a declining fraction of the total area and population was dominated by the military, and by 1928 only six Latin-American countries containing but 15 percent of the total population were ruled by military regimes. Then, abruptly, following the onset of the world depression in 1930, the trend was reversed. There occurred a striking relapse into militarism. A rough measure of this phenomenon, though not always foolproof, was the number of presidents in uniform. In Argentina, for example, after several decades of civilian rule, eight out of ten presidents between 1930 and 1957 were generals or

* Reprinted from Edwin Lieuwen, "Militarism and Politics in Latin America," *The Role of the Military in Underdeveloped Countries,* John J. Johnson, ed., pp. 131-132, 134-136, by permission of Princeton University Press. Copyright © 1962 by the RAND Corporation.

colonels. In those countries which had never developed a civilian tradition in politics, like the republics of the Caribbean and Central America, the military tradition not only continued but was reinforced.

By 1936 half of Latin America was ruled by governments predominantly military in character. Armed-forces regimes were frozen in power during most of World War II. Toward the end of the war the discrediting of military fascism and all forms of totalitarianism helped bring on a noticeable thaw in Latin America. By 1947 only seven out of twenty governments were headed by army officers. Then, following the outbreak of the Korean War, there occurred a new upsurge in military rule. The twentieth-century high was reached in 1954 when thirteen of twenty Latin-American republics were ruled by military presidents.

This reemergence of the armed forces upon the Latin-American political scene, this sudden reversal of definite trends away from military rule was a consequence of the progressive crumbling of the traditional order during the twentieth century. In the resulting political chaos, the armed forces were provoked to intervene against newly articulate groups who were threatening the *status quo*. The motives and justifications of the armed forces varied. Devoted professionals intervened in the name of their legitimate duty to preserve internal order. Latent militarists were motivated only by political ambitions. Officers with idealistic leanings believed it their duty to promote social justice. In some cases, such as Argentina in 1930 and Peru in 1948, the armed forces took over at the behest of the beleaguered civilian oligarchy. In others they acted on behalf of rising popular forces, as in Guatemala in 1944 and Venezuela in 1945. In Colombia, in 1953, the army took over when a stalemate developed in the battle among competing civilian forces. In El Salvador, after 1930, the strength of the civilian oligarchy declined without a concomitant growth in responsible labor and middle-class groups. Accordingly, power went by default to the army, the only organized and disciplined force available for administering the affairs of the nation. . . .

Essential to an understanding of the social significance

of the developments described above is a close examination of the role of the military leaders themselves. For, as might be expected, Latin America's twentieth century economic, social, and political metamorphosis was clearly mirrored in the officer corps. The dramatic struggle that occurred between the old and the new, the farm and the city, and the partisans of the traditional oligarchy and the supporters of the emergent forces resulted in institutional upheavals in the Latin-American armed forces as far-reaching and profound as those that occurred in civilian society.

After World War I there began to appear in the lower echelons of the officer corps increasing numbers of representatives from the rising urban middle groups. The sons of industrialists, bureaucrats, and urban professional men began to acquire the educational background and the modern, progressive outlook that made them superior cadets in the military academies. As in the past, men who chose a career-in-arms continued to come from the middle class, but the military representatives of these new urban groups, unlike the traditionally rural-oriented officer, had no strong ties with either the landed oligarchy or the church hierarchy. Consequently, they had, at least initially, little enthusiasm for perpetuating the role of the armed forces as a guarantor of the traditional social order.

The social identification of the new-type officer with the urban groups where he originated was probably the fundamental cause of the junior-officer uprisings that began to occur in Latin America's armies in the second quarter of the twentieth century. In general, the conflict was between the old and the new generation, between the generals, on the one hand, and the majors, captains, and lieutenants on the other, with the colonels often pulled in both directions. Such cleavages were not new in Latin America; what was new was the social basis of the split.

Almost invariably, Latin America's twentieth-century popular revolutions were led by the young officers. They were the sponsors of fundamental change and reform, the underminers of traditional institutions, the proponents of public welfare measures. As the leading advocates of militarized, authoritarian states, they were apt to speak scornfully of decadent democracy. Their revolutionary zeal was by no means entirely altruistic for changes they advocated in the makeup and role of the armed forces meant unparalleled opportunities for promotion. Extreme nationalistic policies meant expansion and enrichment of the state apparatus upon which the military was dependent for its income.

Post-1930 militarism, therefore, went much deeper than in the past. It was much more complex as new social forces (labor and middle groups) and new military factors (politically influential navies and air forces) were added. Thus, those who stood for the old-type military dictatorship, backed only by the landed oligarchy and the upper clergy and often favored by foreign investors, had to face an entirely new, modern type of military competitor for political power.

Generally speaking, the new leader did not create the new sources of power. More often than not, the environment called forth the man. Inasmuch as the whole Latin-American milieu was changing, so was the road to power. The new technique was to ride to victory at the head of popular reform movements. The new social philosophy was not primarily the brain child of the leader himself. His articulate expression of popular demands, demands in which he himself often did not believe, was a weapon, a technique utilized for the enhancement of his personal power.

III

IDEOLOGY

There is considerable difference of opinion about the nature of ideology. Talcott Parsons describes it broadly as a "general system of beliefs held in common by the members of a collectivity." [1] According to this general definition, democratic as well as authoritarian systems would have a set of ideological beliefs. Freud sees ideology as a set of rationalizations, and Mosca and Pareto as a set of political myths. Here the irrational and psychological aspects of ideologies are emphasized. Friedrich and Brzezinski, on the other hand, believe that the essence of an ideology is its revolutionary quality. They define ideology as "a reasonably coherent body of ideas concerning practical means of how to change and reform a society, based upon a more or less elaborate criticism of what is wrong with the existing, or antecedent society." [2] This definition has an obvious application to totalitarian ideologies.

In the practice of authoritarian regimes the guide to policy may be pure pragmatism, that is, determined by the *ad hoc* needs of the moment, or it may consist of a formal, systematized ideology. The traditional type of dictator after gaining power by a *coup d'état* is often content to act without reference to an elaborate set of beliefs, and bases his actions on what is immediately necessary to preserve his power. The new type of authoritarian leader needs a set of goals to justify to the masses, on whom his support rests in part, the concentration of power and the sacrifices which they are called upon to

[1] Talcott Parsons, *The Social System,* 1951, p. 349.
[2] Carl J. Friedrich and Zbigniew K. Brzezinski, *Totalitarian Dictatorship and Autocracy,* Harvard University Press, 1956, p. 74.

make in the name of social change. These goals are usually presented in the form of an ideology which serves both to galvanize and cement together the people. In this case, the ideology may be after the fact, that is, it may be a set of beliefs developed after the seizure of power as a means of consolidating and perpetuating power. The "Justicialismo" of Perón of Argentina and Nasser's "Arab Socialist Unity" are such *post hoc* ideologies. On the other hand, Marxism was a fully developed doctrine which antedated the 1917 revolution and acted as a guide not only to the revolution itself, but to the system established thereafter.

Schwartz sharpens the question of the relation of ideology to power in practice. One extreme is that practice is dictated by the ideological blueprint. The other extreme is that practice is determined by power considerations alone with ideology subordinated to the role of convenient or even cynical façade. The most generally accepted position, and that of Schwartz himself, is that power considerations and ideology are held in uneasy tension as determinants of policy. This uneasy tension inevitably leads to the erosion of revolutionary ideologies. However, Brzezinski, using communism as an example, points out the many self-perpetuating aspects inherent in ideologies which are conducive to their continuing vitality.

Communism as the example *par excellence* of revolutionary ideologies has many built-in problems. While not all revolutionary ideologies are totalitarian, and while Marxism itself was not totalist, Marx planted the seed which enabled communism to become so when he maintained that he had discovered the *laws* of society much as physical scientists had discovered the laws of nature. Khrushchev made this clear when he said: "Yes, we are firmly convinced of the complete and final triumph of communism. This confidence stems from the knowledge of the laws of the development of society discovered by Marx, Engels and Lenin, which have the same force as the laws of nature, in the sense that they operate objectively." [3] According to the laws of social change found by Marx and Engels, each stage of history must have its

[3] N. K. Khrushchev, *Soviet News,* Jan. 11, 1962, No. 4594, p. 21.

own ideology because men's ideas are determined by their material existence, that is, by the mode of production under which they live. "Does it require deep intuition to comprehend that men's ideas, views, and conceptions, in one word, man's consciousness, changes with every change in the conditions of his material existence, in his social relations and in his social life?—when people speak of ideas that revolutionise society, they do but express the fact that within the old society the elements of a new one have been created, and that the dissolution of the old ideas keeps even pace with the dissolution of the old conditions of existence." [4] Lenin in *What Is To Be Done?* uses the "laws" as a guide for revolutionary action, and pushes Marxism still further in the direction of totalitarianism by insisting that any deviation "in the slightest degree" must not be tolerated.

If ideological dogma is posited in the form of laws but at the same time history must march on, communism is presented with a serious problem: to be both pure and flexible. The solution, as Khrushchev has pointed out, is to consider Marxism a "living, creative doctrine," adapted and enriched by Lenin and others. "Dogmatism," the mechanical application of the words of Marx and Lenin to any circumstance, has become a serious Soviet epithet. The theory of creative adaptation permitted Lenin to interject into communist ideology the concept of the Party as authoritative vanguard of the proletariat, and Stalin the reintroduction of wages on a piecework basis.

If creative adaptation raises a serious theoretical question when applied within a single country, the problem becomes almost insurmountable when it is applied universally to all of the communist countries. Marx-Leninism is one thing, ideologically speaking, but Marx-Lenin-Maoism is quite another. Mao Tse-tung from the early days of communism in China had insisted that Marx-Leninism was the arrow, but it must be aimed to hit the target of the Chinese revolution. Even after defeating Chiang Kai Shek on the mainland in 1949, the Chinese leaders continue to maintain, as seen in the speech of Liu Shao-ch'i of 1961, that the universal truth

[4] Karl Marx and Friedrich Engels, *Manifesto of the Communist Party.*

of Marxism-Leninism must be adapted to the concrete conditions of China. The communes and the "New Democracy" based on a four-class alliance were such adaptations. Adapting ideology to local circumstances may be creative, but it plays havoc with the purity and universalism of the ideology as a whole.

The terms "decay" and "erosion" of ideological purity are used with regard to the universality of application, though not by communists, to be sure. Chou En-lai expressed the dilemma at the Soviet Party Congress in 1961:

> This unity of ours is cemented by common ideals and a common cause; it has been strengthened and developed in joint struggles against our common enemy and it is based on Marxism-Leninism and proletarian internationalism. This unity of ours has stood the test of time; no force can destroy it. Our Socialist camp comprising twelve fraternal countries is a single entity, from the Korean Democratic People's Republic to the German Democratic Republic, from the Democratic Republic of Viet-nam to the Albanian People's Republic. We Socialist countries and we Communist Parties of all countries support and co-operate with each other in a brotherly way, on the basis of independence and full equality. We must unite very well and cherish our unity like the apple of the eye and there should absolutely not be any words or deeds that harm this unity (applause).
>
> We hold that if a dispute or difference unfortunately arises between fraternal parties or fraternal countries, it should be resolved patiently in the spirit of proletarian internationalism and on the principles of equality and unanimity through consultation[5]

This remark, while emphasizing the need for intra-communist unity, was a rebuke to Khrushchev for his ideological attack on Albania. Furthermore, in speaking of cooperation among communist countries on the basis of independence and equality, Chou En-lai was rejecting the concept of any member acting as the single, authoritative source of ideological purity.

Lowenthal traces the shift from a monolithic ideological structure under Stalin which established Soviet pre-

[5] Quoted by Donald S. Zagoria, "Khrushchev's Attack on Albania and Sino-Soviet Relations," *The China Quarterly,* October-December, 1961, p. 17.

eminence to the present polycentrism. Polycentrism may provide flexibility, but it is unlikely to produce ideological purity. For the immediate future the need for cohesion and unity within the communist bloc will probably prevail. However, the eroding aspect of polycentrism will cause increasing difficulties for communism because the other members of the communist bloc now have different models from which to choose, but with a loss of unity and cogency to communist ideology as a universal doctrine.

The non-communist emerging states of Asia, Africa and Latin America have their own ideological problems arising from their particular circumstances. If the nation has had to struggle for independence, the attainment of this major goal reduces the factors producing momentum and unity of purpose. Sukarno's plea for a return to the 1945 constitution and to the fervor, dynamism and motivation of revolutionary days is not unique. Lacking the phased, long-ranged aspects of communist ideology, the new leaders tend to develop an ideology that substitutes the goal of social change for the now-achieved independence in an effort to create a largely non-existent national unity and popular enthusiasm for necessary reforms. The resulting ideology may be spurious, as Almond and Coleman point out, that is, a pseudo-ideology to cloak personal power. More likely, the resulting ideology is eclectic, a pragmatic borrowing from various existing ideologies such as communism, western liberalism, and fascism adapted to local needs. As an example Laqueur indicates that some African states have borrowed communist tactics but not Marx-Leninist theory, and the borrowing may be mixed with such distinctly non-communist doctrines as pan-Africanism or even racialism. Pragmatism rather than dogmatism is characteristic of these eclectic ideologies.

A. THE ROLE OF IDEOLOGY

— 1 —

MOSCOW-PEKING AXIS, STRENGTHS AND STRAINS

Howard L. Boorman, Alexander Eckstein, Philip E. Mosely and Benjamin Schwartz*

Few will quarrel with the notion that economic and power factors play an important role in Sino-Soviet relations. Many observers, however, tend to deprecate the role of ideology in shaping these relations. The assertion that ideology has played and will continue to play a leading role in this partnership is, of course, part of a larger assumption that ideology has played a significant role in the history of Communism in general. Since this proposition is rejected by many, any attempt to deal with the role of ideology in Sino-Soviet relations should be preceded by an expression of views on the larger question.

In the prolonged and complex discussion of this subject over the past decade, the outlines of three overriding points of view can be discerned, at the risk of some over-simplification: the monistic ideological approach, the sociological approach, and the power approach. Perhaps no one view fits neatly into any of these three categories, and within the confines of each of these

* Howard L. Boorman, Alexander Eckstein, Philip E. Mosely and Benjamin Schwartz, *Moscow-Peking Axis, Strengths and Strains,* published for the Council on Foreign Relations by Harper and Brothers, New York, 1957, pp. 112-117. Reprinted by permission.

approaches there have arisen contending schools of thought. Nevertheless, the use of these categories is convenient for purposes of analysis.

The advocates of the monistic ideological approach tend to see in the history of Communism simply the implementation in practice of the ideas of Marx and Lenin. Lenin, Stalin and Mao have simply carried into practice the blueprints of Karl Marx. Like the Communists themselves, those who uphold this approach are inclined to accept the view that Lenin, Stalin (at least until his recent denigration) and Mao have simply "extended and applied" Marx's teachings. For them, there is no problem of the relation of doctrine to practice. They may, to be sure, see in Lenin and Stalin the admixture of certain elements of Russian thought. In any case, however, the development of the Communist world is to be explained in terms of a monolithic Communist religion which directs and informs the actions of its leaders.

In their interpretation of Sino-Soviet relations, supporters of this approach simply point to the Communist religion, shared by the Chinese Communist and Soviet rulers. The common bonds of faith are sufficient to explain the present nature of the alliance and to insure its endurance in the future. Tensions of power, nationalism, differences in historic background, are all outweighed and will continue to be outweighed by the ideological bond. The façade of complete harmony which we find in official writings is to be taken at face value.

The advocates of the sociological approach may differ among themselves in their accounts of the origins of Communist totalitarianism. Some of them may concede that ideology played some role in the beginning. Some of them may insist that the modern Russian social system (as well as the Chinese) is simply the projection into the present of the "oriental" society of the past, while some may explain Communism as the result of the confrontation of economically backward societies with the highly industrialized societies of the West. Whatever their differences on the question of genesis, they all tend to agree that Communist totalitarian society as "a going concern" is held together by iron relations of sociological interdependence and that the vicissitudes of ideology have little to do with the development of the system.

In explaining the evolution of Sino-Soviet relations, the advocates of the sociological approach tend to emphasize the growing basic similarities of social structure in the Soviet Union and in Communist China. They point to the role of the Communist party in both societies, to the emergence of a ruling class of *apparatchiki* in both societies. They point to the totalitarian controls established in both societies and to the present appropriation by the Chinese Communists of the basic Stalinist model of economic development. Indeed at the present time the Chinese Communists seem more genuinely committed to the Stalinist pattern of economic development than even the more stalwart of the Eastern European satellites (although some hesitations and vacillations on this score were manifested at the Chinese Communist Party Congress in September 1956). In general, the sociological approach would insist that, to the extent that the social structures of China and the Soviet Union can be considered identical in all essential respects, the two states can be expected to work together for their common goals in world politics.

Advocates of the power approach emphasize the power interests of ruling groups as the determining factor in both internal and external affairs. The totalitarian social system did not develop spontaneously or inevitably. Over the course of its history the Soviet leadership has confronted numerous situations to which it might have responded by courses of action different from those which it chose. However, the decisions of the ruling groups have been largely motivated by the desire to maximize and make secure their own power within the Communist world and in the world as a whole. All the decisions of the leaders can be explained in terms of the priority of power, and totalitarianism is the consequence of their highly successful efforts. Again according to this view, the vicissitudes of ideology, as such, play no dynamic role in shaping the course of events.

In dealing with Sino-Soviet relations some of the advocates of this approach are inclined to explain Sino-Soviet

relations in terms of direct organizational control of the
Chinese Communist government by the Kremlin. Those
who reject this explanation and doubt the existence of
direct control tend, of course, to stress the shared power
interests of Communist China and the Soviet Union. It is
not difficult to itemize a list of such common interests.
Communist China and the Soviet Union probably share
an interest in ejecting American influence from Asia in
general, and from Japan in particular. They probably
both desire to see Vietnam and Korea drawn completely
into the Communist orbit. On the side of factors which
tend to bind Peking to Moscow, it has been urged by
some that a relatively weak China cannot afford to be
hostile to a powerful Soviet Union with which it shares
an exposed border several thousand miles long. Finally,
since Mao's promulgation of the policy of "leaning to one
side," China has become increasingly dependent on the
Soviet Union for economic and military support. All these
power factors taken together are, from this point of view,
sufficient to explain and predict the nature of the Sino-
Soviet alliance.

While the ideological approach in its monistic form
seems oversimplified, the evolution of ideology has, in
fact, played a crucial role in shaping events within the
Communist world. It is possible to assert both that the
general tendency has been toward the disintegration of
Marxist-Leninist ideology and that ideology has continued
to be of basic importance even in its process of disintegration. One may accept without reservation the contention
that, ever since Lenin began to use Marxism as a "guide
to action," whenever actual circumstances have contra-
dicted some basic point of doctrine, the doctrine has
either been discarded as being unessential or has passed
over from the category of an operational concept to the
status of an empty verbal formula while some new "theoretical analysis" has been spun to rationalize the situation. With Lenin, the notion that the inexorable forces of
the mode of production would themselves lead the workers to emancipate themselves; that the economic situation
of the workers would directly create in them a proper
Socialist mentality; that capitalism would collapse at its
highest point of development; that the bourgeois revolu-

tion would be led by the bourgeoisie—all these commonly accepted Marxist notions were simply discarded when they ran athwart the exigencies of current political demands. Lenin was, of course, extremely resourceful in devising new "theoretical analyses" to account for these and other shifts. Later, when the notion that a Socialist revolution in backward Russia must be accompanied by a proletarian revolution in the West had ceased to have operational consequences, the theory of "socialism in one country" was devised to plaster over this decay in doctrine.

In spite of this steady decay, elements of ideology have continued to shape the Communist world in complex and subtle ways, and on many levels. If it is, indeed, a fact that the ideology has been disintegrating, this is in itself a fact of enormous consequences. The image which leaps to mind is that of a retreating glacier flowing into the sea. Huge chunks of the glacier fall off. The glacier, however, continues to flow and to shape the terrain over which it flows. The fact that the ideology is disintegrating does not preclude the possibility that residual elements of ideology continue to shape the world image of Communist ruling groups. It does not mean that these groups are indifferent to the process of decay or can ever afford to be indifferent even from the point of view of the power which they exercise or claim.

One of the difficulties is that the term "an ideology" suggests an organic, synthetic whole. Before it underwent its Leninist transformation, Marxism did, indeed, constitute a grandiose, albeit unstable, synthesis of nineteenth-century strands of thought. As Professor Gerschenkron states the dilemma, "it is tempting to suggest that in a very real sense the advent of the Bolsheviks to power spelled the end of Marxist ideology." If he simply means that Marxism as an architectonic structure was destroyed, one might be inclined to agree. If he means that elements and combinations of elements drawn from the Marxist-Leninist complex of ideas have not continued to shape the Communist world, this would seem to be serious over-simplification. After all, in the course of his own manipulations of doctrine, Lenin himself developed a derivative or secondary body of doctrine of his own, which subsequently came to form a part of the orthodoxy under the name of Leninism.

— 2 —

IDEOLOGY AND POWER IN SOVIET POLITICS

Zbigniew K. Brzezinski*

But this process of erosion is at the present time balanced by certain pressures in the opposite direction, which reassert and even revitalize the ideology. . . .

In the Soviet Union, several established commitments act as powerful counterforces and protect the ideology from erosion. The most important of these is the institutional commitment in the form of the ruling party. Not much needs to be said about this most important factor. If the ideology were to fade, particularly among the membership, the power of the Party would be threatened, even though ritualization could delay the disintegration. The upper echelons of the Party are very conscious of this. The steps taken by Khrushchev to re-establish the role of the Party in Soviet society and the recent measures adopted to invigorate the ideological indoctrination of the population at large suggest that the Party is determined to maintain ideological consciousness in its ranks. In the foreseeable future, there is little reason to doubt its capacity to do so.

The institutional commitment to ideology is backed by a personal commitment. To individuals like Khrushchev, the ideology is the source of their insight into reality, a

* Zbigniew K. Brzezinski, *Ideology and Power in Soviet Politics,* Frederick A. Praeger, Inc., New York, 1962, pp. 134, 135-138. Reprinted by permission.

conscious treasure to be guarded against pollution (unless by themselves, which is a different problem), the basic course of their education (*Rabfak,* in Khrushchev's case), and the emotional source for their personal sense of life. The present generation of Soviet leaders—men in their early sixties—came of age during the latter stages of the civil war and matured during the NEP and the Stalinist transformation of Russia. Their first contact with the ideology came at a time when the Party was still intensely preoccupied with ideological issues and was attempting— through debate, deviations, and purges—to determine what course to pursue in building a new society. Even a simple young member like Khrushchev, for example, could not avoid involvement and had to make his choice. Ideology, in the 1920's was an important matter, even if one were to focus merely on the power struggles that were taking place. Khrushchev's experience in this period was bound to leave with him a lasting awareness that there is a "correct" and an "erroneous" path and that the Party must always remain conscious of this. In a decade or so from now, and maybe sooner, a new generation of Soviet leaders will come to the fore. The men who are now in their fifties—e.g., Brezhnev and Kozlov—were twenty when Stalin undertook his collectivization drive and defeated all opposition, and they were in their mid-twenties when the Party experienced its great purge. They faced no alternatives. To them, power equaled ideology. The road forward was simple, firmly charted, and not subject to discussion. To such a generation, ideology may be less a matter of conscious preoccupation. This may make them in some ways much more defenseless against unarticulated social processes that quietly erode the ideology. Nevertheless, the habits of thought and the personal experience of the Soviet leaders will act as a braking element on the force stimulating erosion.

Broad social commitment is another "defensive" element. As values become socially ingrained, they resist new values. The reconstruction of Soviet society on the basis of the ideology and the indoctrination of many decades has created a social residue that will resist the intrusion of new ideas, even though the intellectually alert elements may be drawn by them. The influence on the latter can be effective only if they either penetrate the Party or succeed in infusing the society with new notions. Given the nature of the Soviet society, the task for the carriers of new ideas is not easy, unless a major crisis should shake its stability. In some ways, it can even be argued that urbanization and industrialization, achieved within an ideological context and by an ideologically motivated movement, will tend to perpetuate the role of ideology. First, they institutionalize an environment that is based on the ideological aspirations and in time begins to act as a buffer for that ideology; second, through a very tangible sense of achievement, they create a widespread acceptance of the ideology, which, even if lacking its original revolutionary zeal, becomes gradually more pervading; third, the nature of a modern industrial society, which is based on social ownership and has severely limited individual initiative, requires a continuous articulation of societal goals to help preserve the broadly accepted purpose. These factors together are inimical to a rapid erosion of the ideology. Finally, action commitment revitalizes the ideology. Action provokes reaction and breeds hostility and conflict and thereby intensifies belief, steeled by trial. Action crowned by success strengthens the ideology even more. In so far as the masses are concerned, the Soviet leadership has been making strenuous efforts to identify its successes in launching Sputniks or achieving a higher rate of growth with its ideology. Indeed, it may be one of the ironies of the Soviet version of Communism that Soviet military preponderance might become an element that retrenches and intensifies ideological belief.

B. IDEOLOGY IN THE COMMUNIST BLOC

— 1 —

MARXISM AS CREATIVE DOCTRINE
Nikita Khrushchev*

Question: Do you agree with the opinion that Karl Marx, if he were able to rise from his grave and see with his own eyes how our society has changed as compared with 1848, as a result of the appearance of nuclear weapons, rockets, new technology, automation of production and mass means of communication, would on many points speak differently from what he said in the Communist Manifesto?

Answer: The genius of Marx and Engels enabled them to look far into the future, to discover the basic laws of the development of human society and define the most characteristic features of communism. Their greatest merit is that they founded the scientific theory of communism and thus indicated the only correct road to the destruction of the material and spiritual bondage in which the oppressed peoples languished.

Tremendous changes have taken place both in science and technology and in the development of society in the hundred years and more that have passed since the appearance of the Communist Manifesto. The world of today is far from what it was in Marx's time. A new social system, socialism, has emerged and is developing successfully; the world system of colonialism has collapsed. Certain changes have also been experienced by capitalism, which entered the imperialist stage of development at the

* *Soviet News,* January 11, 1962, No. 4594, p. 22.

beginning of the 20th century. But the essence of capitalism as a society based on the exploitation of man by man remains what it was in the time of Marx, while the internal contradictions inherent in capitalism have become still more acute.

The opponents of Marxism are seeking to prove that capitalism has transformed itself into something between capitalism and socialism. They even replace the very word "capitalism" with such terms as "welfare state," "people's capitalism," "economic humanism," and so on. The opponents of Marxism try to present the important changes taking place in science and technology as the beginning of the new epoch of prospering capitalism.

But the game of fine words cannot refute the obvious facts: scientific and technical progress does not and cannot change the essence of capitalism as a social formation. The development of science and technology has not abolished antagonistic classes and class differences in capitalist society. The worker, who has exchanged the spade for the excavator, remains subjected to ruthless capitalist exploitation, and this exploitation is absolutely inevitable under capitalism. This is a law of the capitalist social system.

Marxism is a living creative doctrine, and dogmatism and obsolete formulas are alien to it. After Marx, Lenin enriched Marxism with new highly important theoretical conclusions. The entire experience of our time, the emergence and development of the socialist community and the growth of its might, and the extensive spread of the ideas of socialism and communism throughout the world corroborate irrefutably Lenin's words that the doctrine of Marx is all-powerful because it is correct.

The communists of the Soviet Union, developing the ideas of Marx and Lenin creatively, have worked out a new party programme. The implementation of this programme will make it possible to fulfil mankind's age-old dream of a society without classes, without social and national oppression, without wars. If Marx were among us communists of the mid-twentieth century today, he would see the triumphant march of communism in the world and he would rejoice at the practical realization of the great ideas of the Communist Manifesto and say with pride: "Yes, the ideas of communism live on and are winning through; the future belongs to them."

— 2 —

WHAT IS TO BE DONE?
V. I. Lenin*

Since there can be no talk of an independent ideology being developed by the masses of the workers in the process of their movement then *the only choice is:* Either bourgeois, or Socialist ideology. There is no middle course (for humanity has not created a "third" ideology, and, moreover, in a society torn by class antagonisms there can never be a non-class or above-class ideology). Hence, to belittle Socialist ideology *in any way,* to *deviate from it in the slightest degree* means strengthening bourgeois ideology. There is a lot of talk about spontaneity, but the *spontaneous* development of the labour movement leads to its becoming subordinated to bourgeois ideology, it means developing *according to the programme* of the *Credo,* for the spontaneous labour movement is pure and simple trade unionism, is *Nur-Gewerkschaftlerei,* and trade unionism means the ideological subordination of the workers to the bourgeoisie. Hence, our task, the task of Social-Democracy, is to *combat spontaneity,* to *divert* the labour movement, with its spontaneous trade-unionist striving, from under the wing of the bourgeoisie, and to bring it under the wing of revolutionary Social-Democracy.

* V. I. Lenin, *What Is To Be Done?,* International Publishers, 1929, pp. 40-41.

— 3 —

CORRECTING UNORTHODOX TENDENCIES (1942)

Mao Tse-tung*

In shooting the arrow, you must have a target to aim at. The relation between Marxism-Leninism and the Chinese revolution is the same as between the arrow and the target. However, some comrades are shooting arrows without a target, shooting them at random. Such people can easily harm the revolutionary cause. Some comrades merely take the arrow in hand, twist it back and forth, and say again and again in praise, "excellent arrow, excellent arrow," but are never willing to shoot it. This type of person is an antique connoisseur who has hardly any relationship with the revolution. The arrow of Marxism-Leninism must be used to hit the target of the Chinese revolution. If it were otherwise, why would we want to study Marxism-Leninism? Is it because we have not digested our millet that we read a book to relieve indigestion? Why has our Party School decided to study Marxism-Leninism? If this problem is not clearly understood, the theoretical level of the Party can never be raised nor can the Chinese revolution succeed.

Our comrades must understand that we do not study Marxism-Leninism because it is pleasing to the eye, nor because it has some mystical value, like the doctrines of the Taoist priests who ascend Mao-shan (*Chü-yung,*

* Reprinted by permission of the publishers from Conrad Brandt, Benjamin Schwartz and John K. Fairbank, *A Documentary History of Chinese Communism*, Harvard University Press and George Allen and Unwin, Ltd., 1952, pp. 384-385.

Kiangsu) to learn, so they can subdue the devils and evil spirits. Marxism-Leninism has no decorative value, nor has it mystical value. It is only extremely useful. It seems that, right up to the present, quite a few have regarded Marxism-Leninism as a ready-made panacea: once you have it, you can cure all your ills with little effort. This is a type of childish blindness, and we must start a movement to enlighten these people. Those who regard Marxism-Leninism as religious dogma show this type of blind ignorance. We must tell them openly, "Your dogma is of no use," or to use an impolite phrase, "Your dogma is less useful than excrement." We see that dog excrement can fertilize the fields, and man's can feed the dog. And dogmas? They can't fertilize the fields, nor can they feed a dog. Of what use are they? (Laughter) Comrades! You know that the object of such talk is to ridicule those who regard Marxism-Leninism as dogma, to frighten and awaken them, to inculcate in them a correct attitude towards Marxism-Leninism. Marx, Lenin, Engels, and Stalin have repeatedly said, "our doctrine is not dogma; it is a guide to action." Of all things, these people forget this most important sentence. Theory and practice can be combined only if men of the CCP take the standpoints, concepts, and methods of Marxist-Leninism, apply them to China, and create a theory from conscientious research on the realities of the Chinese revolution and Chinese history. If we merely verbalize about union but do not practice union in our actions, we can talk for a hundred years and still not benefit. Since we are opposed to subjective and *ex-parte* views on problems, we must break through the subjective and one-sided nature of dogmatism.

— 4 —

ON COALITION GOVERNMENT
(1945)

Mao Tse-tung*

Some people wonder if the Communists, once in power, will establish a dictatorship by the proletariat and a one-party system, as they have done in Russia. Our answer is that a New Democratic state of a union of several democratic classes is different in principle from a socialist state of a proletarian dictatorship. China, throughout the period of her New Democratic system, cannot and should not have a system of government of the character of a one-class dictatorship or a one-party autocracy. We have no reason not to co-operate with political parties, social groups, or individuals, outside the CP, who adopt a co-operative, but not a hostile attitude. Russian history has created the Russian system. There the social system in which man exploits man has been abolished; the newest form of democracy—the socialist political, economic, and cultural system has been established; all anti-socialist political parties have been thrown out by the people, who support only the Bolshevik Party. To the Russians, such a system is completely necessary and rational, but even in Russia where the Bolshevik Party is the only political party, the governmental authority is invested in a union of workers, peasants, and intellectuals, or in an alliance of Party members and non-Party members; it is also not

* Reprinted by permission of the publishers from Conrad Brandt, Benjamin Schwartz and John K. Fairbank, *A Documentary History of Chinese Communism,* Harvard University Press and George Allen and Unwin, Ltd., 1952, pp. 305-306.

one in which only workers or the bolsheviks can work in the governmental organs. Chinese history will create the Chinese system. A special type, a New Democratic type of state with a union of several democratic classes will be produced, which will be entirely necessary and rational to us and different from the Russian system.

— 5 —

INTEGRATING THEORY WITH PRACTICE

Liu Shao-ch'i*

The history of the Communist Party of China is the history of the ever closer integration of the universal truth of Marxism-Leninism with the concrete practice of the Chinese revolution. Comrade Mao Tse-tung has said, "The victories of the revolution and construction in our country are all victories of Marxism-Leninism. The ideological principle consistently followed by our Party is to link closely the theory of Marxism-Leninism and the practice of the Chinese revolution."

In every historical period of our Party it has been the leader of our Party, Comrade Mao Tse-tung, who has stood at the very forefront and who has been the most able in integrating the universal truth of Marxism-Leninism with the concrete practice of China. (*Prolonged, stormy applause.*)

Confronted with the extreme complexity of the Chinese revolution, Comrade Mao Tse-tung correctly posed and resolved a series of theoretical and tactical problems, thus enabling the Chinese revolution to steer clear of one shoal after another and to capture one position after another.

* *Peking Review*, July 7, 1961, Nos. 26 and 27, pp. 7-11.

Proceeding from a concrete analysis of the classes in Chinese society, Comrade Mao Tse-tung charted the historical course of the Chinese revolution. He pointed out that the Chinese revolution must advance in two steps; the first was the people's democratic revolution and the second, the socialist revolution.

The enemies of China's democratic revolution were imperialism, feudalism and bureaucrat-capitalism and they were very powerful. But the latent revolutionary strength of the Chinese people was even more powerful. The peasantry constituted the overwhelming majority of the population of our country. By forming a solid worker-peasant alliance with the broad masses of peasants and by uniting on the basis of this alliance with the various nationalities and the people of all revolutionary strata, the Chinese working class was able to defeat these powerful enemies. Comrade Mao Tse-tung correctly resolved the problems of the peasant movement, armed struggle, the united front and the building of the Party; these were the most fundamental problems of China's democratic revolution. . . .

Guided by the general line and the various specific policies for the period of transition to socialism which were laid down by the Party's Central Committee headed by Comrade Mao Tse-tung, our socialist revolution may be said to have proceeded comparatively rapidly and smoothly.

On the socialist transformation of agriculture: We applied Lenin's theory of the worker-peasant alliance under the dictatorship of the proletariat and his theory of agricultural co-operation; we summed up the experience we gained in our revolutionary base areas in the movement for agricultural mutual aid and co-operation; and in accordance with the concrete conditions of our country after liberation, we relied on the poor peasants and lower middle peasants, united firmly with the rest of the middle peasantry, used various transitional forms and thus enabled our agriculture to change from an individual economy to a socialist collective economy.

On the socialist transformation of the industry and commerce of the national bourgeoisie: We applied Marx's idea that in certain conditions the proletariat may adopt a policy of buying out the bourgeoisie and applied Lenin's ideas concerning the policy of state capitalism under proletarian dictatorship; we summed up our Party's experience of its industrial and commercial policies in the revolutionary base areas; and in accordance with the concrete conditions of our country after liberation, we carried out the combined policy of utilizing, restricting and transforming capitalist industry and commerce and used various forms of state capitalism, ranging from the lower to the higher, in order to achieve this transformation. . . .

Comrade Mao Tse-tung and the Central Committee of our Party applied the Marxist-Leninism theory on socialist construction, drew on the experiences of the Soviet Union and other socialist countries in construction, and on the basis of our experiences in carrying out the First Five-Year Plan formulated the general line for China's socialist construction—the general line of going all out, aiming high and achieving more, faster, better and more economical results in building socialism. (*Applause.*)

What is the basic significance of this general line? It is to utilize to the maximum the enormous potentiality of the socialist system for developing the productive forces of society, to mobilize all the positive factors, to unite with all the forces that can be united with, to put into effect the series of policies of "walking on two legs," to develop our national economy in a planned and proportionate way and at high speed so that our country can change at a comparatively fast rate from a backward into an advanced country. (*Applause.*)

Today our country is still economically backward. Imperialism continues to bully us. The people of our country urgently demand an end to this backwardness. There is not the slightest doubt that our Party's general line for socialist construction conforms to the aspirations of the whole people. (*Applause.*)

Guided by the Party's general line for building socialism, our country has made big leaps forward for three consecutive years from 1958. Meanwhile, in our countryside there have emerged the people's communes formed by agricultural co-operatives joining together. Thus the general line, the big leap forward and the people's commune have become the three red banners that are leading the Chinese people forward. (*Prolonged enthusiastic applause.*) . . .

Comrade Mao Tse-tung has said, "The important thing is to be good at learning." At present the most important task is to unfold a new campaign of study throughout the Party. The primary purpose of this campaign is to help all Party cadres further to understand and grasp the objective laws of China's socialist construction, so that we can build socialism in our country with more, faster, better and more economical results. All Party members and cadres should study conscientiously the basic Marxist-Leninist principles of socialist revolution and socialist construction, study the theoretical and practical problems of China's socialist construction as elucidated by Comrade Mao Tse-tung on the basis of Marxist-Leninist principles, study the general line and the various specific policies of socialist construction as formulated by the Central Committee of the Party, and study the experience in socialist construction of the Soviet Union and other fraternal countries. As for the large number of new Party members, they must in addition be given basic education in Marxism-Leninism and basic knowledge of the Party.

Through this campaign of study all Party cadres should consciously improve their style of work and further develop the traditional Marxist-Leninist style of our Party. To do this, we must, as Comrade Mao Tse-tung has consistently said, learn how to use the theory and method of Marxism-Leninism to make meticulous investigations and studies of the environment and to derive from objective reality the inherent laws, and not imaginary laws, as our guide to action. Comrade Mao Tse-tung pointed out long ago that in order to bring about the victory of the Chinese revolution we must depend on the understanding by Chinese comrades of Chinese conditions. He has stated:

Correct and firm tactics of struggle for the Communist Party can never be produced by a handful of people sitting in a room. They can only be produced in the process of the struggles of the masses, that is to say, they can only be produced through practical experience. For only through practical experience can a correct estimate of the class forces be made, only thus can correct and firm tactics of struggle be produced and the victory of the revolution safeguarded. To this end, we need at all times to understand the conditions in society and to conduct practical investigations.

This is the Marxist-Leninist style of integrating theory with practice, the style of seeking truth from facts.

In the history of our Party, not all cadres have had this style, and much less so at the beginning. In different periods of our country's revolution, there appeared in our Party right or "left" errors, both the result of divorce from reality. Their common characteristics were disregard of the investigation and study of objective reality, failure to understand the concrete conditions of China and the belief that the Chinese revolution could be directed by relying on subjective imagination and impressions of the moment, or by merely adducing isolated quotations from certain books. It is well known that these erroneous tendencies caused setbacks of various kinds to the Chinese revolution. Our comrades must bear this lesson in mind, must in their work adhere to the style of seeking truth from facts as advocated by Comrade Mao Tse-tung, and must prevent or overcome every kind of subjective style.

— 6 —

DIPLOMACY AND REVOLUTION: THE DIALECTICS OF A DISPUTE

Richard Lowenthal*

Thus matters come back to the ultimate issue of ideological authority—of the right to interpret ambiguous principles in a changing situation. Here, the Soviets score a clear but very limited victory: they emerge as the most

* Richard Lowenthal, "Diplomacy and Revolution: The Dialectics of a Dispute," *China Quarterly*, January-March 1961, No. 5, pp. 20-21, 23-24. Reprinted by permission.

successful, but not as the only orthodox interpreters of
the true doctrine. The Soviet Union is hailed as the only
country that, having completed "Socialist construction,"
is engaged in building the "higher stage" of Communism;
the Chinese communes are not even mentioned, and the
Soviet argument that Communist abundance is not possible short of the highest level of technical productivity,
including automation, is hammered home. The CPSU is
unanimously declared to be "the universally recognized
vanguard of the world Communist movement," and its
superior experience in conquering power and transforming society is stated to have fundamental lessons for all
parties; the decisions of its Twentieth Congress in particular are said to have opened a new era for the whole
international movement. But that new era now turns out
to be an era of polycentric autonomy—just as the bolder
spirits thought at the time.

For under the new declaration, the spiritual authority
of the CPSU is not incarnated in the shape which all
doctrinaire authority, and certainly all authority in the
Bolshevik tradition, requires by its nature—the shape of
hierarchical discipline. It is not only that the declaration
repeats the ancient pious formula about the independence
and equality of all Communist parties; it is that it fails to
establish a visible, single centre for their dependence. It
provides for irregular conferences, whether world-wide or
regional, for mutual co-ordination, and for bipartite consultations between any two parties in case of differences.
This may be intended to rule out the circulation of Chinese
attacks on CPSU policy to third parties before they have
raised the matter in Moscow directly; but it does not, on
the face of it, prevent them from broadening the discussion again the next time they fail to get satisfaction in
their direct contact with the "vanguard of the world movement." Clearly, the primacy of the vanguard is no longer
that of an infallible Pope: the rule of *Moscow locuta,
causa finita* is valid no more. For the first time in its forty
years of history, international Communism is entering a
"conciliary" period. . . .

On the other hand, the declaration's recognition of the
Soviet Communist Party as the "vanguard" of the world
movement falls far short of establishing a permanent and

unchallengeable doctrinaire authority, let alone a single centre endowed with disciplinary powers. It even falls far short of the position conceded to the Soviet Union and the Soviet Communist Party at the time of the 1957 Moscow declaration—on Mao Tse-tung's initiative. Then, the Soviet Union was consistently described as being "at the head of the Socialist camp," and Mao publicly went out of his way to speak of the need for a single leader both among Communist states and parties, and to insist that only the Russians could fill both roles.

Now, the Chinese talk quite openly and naturally about the special responsibilities of "the two great Socialist powers," the Soviet Union and China; and in the declaration itself, the vanguard role of the Soviet party is balanced in part by the recognition of the "enormous influence" exerted by the Chinese revolution on the peoples of Asia, Africa and Latin America by its encouraging example to all movements of national liberation. In 1957, the failure to found a new formal international organisation only increased the influence of the large international liaison machinery developed within the secretariat of the central committee of the CPSU, compared with which all bilateral and regional contacts were bound to be of subordinate importance. Now, the failure formally to establish a single centre legitimates the *de facto* existence of two centres in Moscow and Peking, both with world-wide links and without any agreed division of labour, which will continue to cooperate on the basis of the declaration but also to give different advice on the questions it has left open and to compete for influence. And if Moscow is still the stronger power and the older authority, Peking is closer in its type of revolutionary experience and the emotional roots of its anti-colonialist ardour to those parts of the world where the chances of Communist revolution are most promising.

In a long-range view, the relative victory of the Soviets in the 1960 phase of the dispute thus appears less important than the fact that this phase has marked a new stage in their abdication of their former position of exclusive leadership. The reports that the Soviets themselves expressed during the Moscow conference a wish that they should be no longer described as being "at the head of the Socialist camp" may well be true: finding themselves unable any longer to exert effective control over the whole world movement, they may have preferred not to be held responsible for all its actions by their enemies. In a *bloc* containing two great powers, in an international movement based on two great revolutions, such a development was indeed to be expected as soon as important differences appeared between them. But while the two protagonists remain as determined to continue to co-operate as they are unable to settle their disagreements, the result is not a two-headed movement with neatly separated geographic spheres of control, but a truly polycentric one: many Communist parties outside the Soviet *bloc* may in future be able to gain increased tactical independence, based on their freedom of taking aid and advice from both Moscow and Peking, simultaneously or alternately —with all the risks that implies for the future unity of its doctrine and strategy.

The victory of Communism in China, and the subsequent growth of Communist China into a great power, thus appears in retrospect as the beginning of the end of the single-centered Communist movement that Lenin created, and the single-centered Soviet *bloc* that Stalin built. The process took a decisive step forward in 1956, when the Twentieth Congress of the CPSU recognized the existence of a "Socialist world system" and of different roads to power, and when the destruction of the Stalin cult inflicted an irreparable blow on the type of Soviet authority that had depended on the infallibility of the "father of nations." Mao's victory had killed the uniqueness of the Soviet Union; Khrushchev's speech buried the myth built around that uniqueness.

It was at that moment that the spectre of "polycentric Communism" first appeared. But when destalinisation was quickly followed by the crisis of Russia's East European empire, the façade of single-centred unity was restored in the following year with the help of China's prestige and Mao's authority. Now that China herself has brought back the spectre she helped to exorcise three years ago, the process is no longer reversible. This time, polycentric Communism has come to stay.

C. IDEOLOGY IN DEVELOPING COUNTRIES

— 1 —

RES PUBLICA!
ONCE MORE RES PUBLICA!
President Sukarno*

In my speech to install this Constituent Assembly I said, among other things: Let us not imitate: Let us not import and take over liberal democracy, because that system is not in harmony with the soul, the spirit, the identity of the Indonesian Nation, nor is it in harmony with the situation in our country.

But what is in harmony with the Indonesian atmosphere —I said further—is that democratic system where the weaker groups are protected; where the power of the stronger groups is restricted; where the exploitation of weaker groups by stronger ones is prevented.

This means that Indonesian democracy must be a democracy with guidance, or democracy with leadership, it must be guided democracy; thus it must be a democracy which is not based on principles of liberalism.

In my "Conception" to "save the Republic of Indonesia," which I submitted to the judgment of the forum of Indonesian society on February 27, 1957, I said that the democracy we have applied up to now is Western democracy—call it parliamentary democracy if you like.

Because it is not in harmony with the Indonesian atmosphere, excesses are bound to occur when Western

* President Sukarno, *Res Publica! Once More Res Publica!* Ministry of Information, Republic of Indonesia, 1959, pp. 19-21.

democracy is applied, excesses such as misuse of the idea of "opposition" in the political field; violation of discipline and hierarchy in the military field; corruption and other such-like offences in the socio-economic field.

Therefore, to prevent all kinds of difficulties in the executive as well as in the constitutional sphere, it is necessary for us to return to the democracy of the 1945 Constitution. That harmonizes best with the Indonesian atmosphere and is called "democracy led by wise guidance in consultation by representatives"—(*kerakjatan jang dipimpin oleh hikmat kebidjaksanaan dalam permusjawaratan perwakilan*).

What is meant by "democracy led by wise guidance in consultation by representatives"?

This I intend to explain in discussing the following main idea: THE 1945 CONSTITUTION IS A BETTER GUARANTEE FOR THE IMPLEMENTATION OF THE PRINCIPLE OF GUIDED DEMOCRACY. GUIDED DEMOCRACY IS DEMOCRACY.

The Government has given the following definitions of guided democracy:

1. Guided democracy is democracy or, in the words of the 1945 Constitution, "democracy led by wise guidance in consultation by representatives."

2. Guided democracy is not dictatorship; it differs from centralist democracy as well as from the liberal democracy we have practiced up to now.

3. Guided democracy is a democracy which harmonizes with the personality and the outlook of the Indonesian Nation.

4. Guided democracy is democracy in all affairs of the State and Society covering the political, economic and social spheres.

5. The substance of leadership in guided democracy is consultation; however, it is that kind of consultation which is "led by wise guidance" (*dipimpin oleh hikmat kebidjaksanaan*), not one which is led by "debates and manoeuvres, ending in a trial of strength and the calculation of the figures for and against." The outcome of "representative consultations led by wise guidance" is then submitted for implementation to a President, who, incidentally, is also elected by way of consultations. To carry into effect

the results of these consultations, the President appoints good and capable persons as his assistants, but the President remains individually (not collectively with his assistants) responsible to the Consultative Body of People's representatives (*Madjelis Permusjawaratan Perwakilan Rakjat*). Further, in the day-to-day conduct of State affairs (whose outlines are defined by that Consultative Body) the President must work together with the People's Representative Council, the Parliament (*Dewan Perwakilan Rakjat*). Such cooperation must also be practiced by means of "consultation led by wise guidance," and must not give priority to debates and manoeuvres which may lead to the dissolution of an entire Cabinet—things which are not possible under the 1945 Constitution.

6. Opposition in the sense of expressing sound and constructive opinions is a necessity under guided democracy; the important thing is the manner of deliberation in the representative consultations led by wise guidance.

7. Guided democracy is a means, not an end.

8. The object of implementing guided democracy is to arrive at a just and prosperous society, full of material and spiritual happiness, in harmony with the ideals of Indonesia's Independence Proclamation of August 17, 1945.

9. Since it is a means, guided democracy also recognizes freedom of thought and of expression, but within certain limits, i.e., the limits imposed by the safety of the State, the interest of the people at large, the national identity, morality and responsibility to God.

— 2 —

THE POLITICS
OF THE DEVELOPING AREAS
Gabriel A. Almond
and James S. Coleman*

Ideological life in Latin America has been characterized by an ambivalence between the extremes of authoritarian thought, still deeply embedded in the area, and the ideological bases of democracy and constitutional government, which, after all, provided the foundations upon which the independent states of the area were erected. This ambivalence has taken a number of forms. The most common of them is an eclecticism, which may appear curious to the North American, in which elements of authoritarianism and constitutionalism—often logically incompatible with each other—are combined in a single system. Thus a strong dictator may preside over an arrangement equipped with a democratically oriented written constitution; a small landowning oligarchy may rule a state while vigorously proclaiming the rights of man; and Church and State may be united in a system espousing some philosophical elements of the French Revolution.

New ideological ingredients have been introduced into Latin America in more recent times, particularly during the late nineteenth and early twentieth centuries. Marxism is among the most significant of these. Socialism came to the area in the 1890's. Socialist parties remain active in most of the countries, particularly in Argentina, Chile,

* Reprinted from *The Politics of the Developing Areas* by Gabriel A. Almond and James S. Coleman (eds.), 1960, pp. 490-492, by permission of Princeton University Press.

Ecuador, and Uruguay. In general, the Socialists have been noteworthy for their participation in programs directed toward land reform, the emergence of a labor movement, and an accelerated rate of secularization. Communism, another ideological child of Marxism, also has its organized adherents in the area. The most important Communist parties are to be found in Argentina, Brazil, Chile, Colombia, Cuba, Guatemala, and Uruguay. Finally, Fascism, introduced into Latin America in the 1930's, has also produced ideological movements there—notably the nationalist organizations which were embraced by the Peronistas in Argentina, the Integralistas of Brazil, and the Sinarquista and PAN of Mexico.

The Latin American tendency toward ideological eclecticism—combining elements of diverse philosophical systems to form a new unit—has contributed to two types of phenomena in the area. The first of these involves native ideological movements which contain ingredients borrowed from the sources discussed above. Many of these movements, for example, have taken some elements of Marxism, joined them with ingredients indigenous to Latin America, and produced ideological systems that have often acquired great political strength. The two leading illustrations of this in contemporary Latin America are the Apristas of Peru and the PRI of Mexico. Thus, the ideological base of Aprismo is essentially a mixture of the nationalism of the indigenous Peruvian Indian, the anticlericalism of the French Revolution, and a demand for land reform and a resistance to imperialism stemming from Marxism. Similarly, the doctrine of the Mexican PRI is compounded of Indian nationalism, eighteenth-century French anticlericalism, and those elements of Marxism contributing to land reform, a strong interest in the development of a labor movement, and opposition to imperialism.

A second Latin American phenomenon encouraged by the tendency toward eclecticism is the development of spurious ideological movements. These borrow small fragments—often only slogans—of established systems of ideas and incorporate them into new movements. It is characteristic of the spurious phenomenon—and this is what distinguishes it from the native ideological move-

ment—that it is a superficial borrowing of the vocabulary
and slogans, rather than the ideas, of diverse philosophies;
in the typical spurious system there is little or no consistent
political thought. Essentially a political tool, the spurious
ideology is often "used by a leader in order to enlist
greater obedience among his followers or to obtain new
otherwise inaccessible recruits, but the leader does not
himself believe in the ideology propagated by him, unless
this happens unbeknownst to himself—having repeated
the same words once too often, he finally believes in
them."

Regardless of their logical and philosophical indefensi-
bility, spurious ideologies have been of growing importance in Latin America, and movements of this type have
seized power in a number of the countries of the area.

— 3 —

COMMUNISM AND NATIONALISM IN TROPICAL AFRICA
Walter Z. Laqueur*

According to official Communist sources, there are no
"Marxist-Leninist mass parties" at present in Africa south
of the Sahara—with the sole exception of one on the
island of Réunion. . . . There are, of course, individual
Communists in many African countries, and the intention
to establish Communist Parties at some future date is
clear. It is apparently thought, however, that at present
Communists should work through other political move-

* Walter Z. Laqueur, "Communism and Nationalism in Tropical Africa," *Foreign Affairs*, Vol. 39, No. 4, July 1961,
  pp. 611-618. Reprinted by permission.

ments as well as through front organizations and trade unions. In present circumstances, the existence of official Communist parties would probably be more of a handicap than an advantage, given the reluctance of Africans to get involved with super-national movements and ideologies. Moreover, there are probably no more than a handful of Communists in the whole African continent whose political education and judgment come up to Moscow's requirements. In view of the many past disappointments with African fellow travellers, who for a while cooperated with the Communists but then turned against them, or simply drifted away, it is thought preferable to delay the recognition of official Communist parties until more evidence has been received about the quality of the candidates for Communist representation and leadership.

Communism in 1961 means different things to different people. Afro-Communism as it now emerges has not very much in common with the theories of Karl Marx, not even in the modified form in which they have been applied in politically and economically backward countries. Afro-Communism represents above all a means of gaining political power for a small group of intellectuals. In foreign policy its protagonists stand for close collaboration with the Soviet bloc and/or China. On the domestic scene it implies agrarian reform, frequently a foreign trade monopoly and central planning, a one-party dictatorship and the gradual indoctrination of the population with some kind of official ideology. It hardly needs to be demonstrated that such revolutionary technique may be very efficient both in gaining power and in maintaining it; of this China will serve as an example. But it is equally obvious that the net result is a system that has very little in common with Marxism as it was originally conceived. It is in effect a new political phenomenon that can be only partly explained by reference to developments in the past, or in other parts of the world.

Clearly Afro-Communism cannot be equated with Communism as known in Russia or the West, but there are also important differences between Afro-Communism and Communism in Asia. The leaders of the Chinese, Korean or Indonesian parties were closely connected with the Comintern or Cominform for decades; they have had a thorough training in the essentials of Leninism, they have acquired the specific mental make-up of leading members of a very powerful sect, and they subject themselves to party discipline and "proletarian internationalism." In short, leaders like Mao or Ho Chi-Minh modelled themselves on the "ideal type" of the Russian Bolshevik of the 1920s.

The representatives of Afro-Communism, on the other hand, belong to a much younger generation. They grew up at a time when Communism had become much more powerful, but its ideological and psychological impact much lighter—and when various centers of Communist power had come into being. Their familiarity with the theory of Marxism-Leninism is often superficial, restricted in most cases to some knowledge of its more practical aspects such as political organization and planning, and of course a nodding acquaintance with the Leninist theory of imperialism. These are not the strong and silent heroes who had to fight for many years in conditions of illegality. Independence and power came to them on the whole rather easily; as in Guinea, they sometimes received it on a platter. Their beliefs are, in short, less deeply rooted and they are very unlike the intransigent "Old Bolsheviks" with their iron discipline and their unending ideological squabbles. The rudimentary political training they have received may give them an advantage over their political rivals and competitors, but it does not make them Communists in the sense of the word accepted in the West; at most they are Communists of a new type. This is not to split theoretical hairs or to stick unduly to ideological niceties; it has important and far-reaching implications.

It means, for instance, that nationalism, Pan-Africanism and even racialism play an important part in the attitude of these leaders. In Moscow their *nationalisme communisant* is regarded with great indulgence as a transitional phenomenon that will in due time give way to the real thing. (No such tolerance is shown to Tito, an old Comrade who ought to know better.) But it is highly doubtful whether this "transitional phenomenon" will really end as the Communists expect. The Afro-Communists have their own ideas about what ought to be done in their continent, and they are not overawed by the authority of Lenin or the experience of Communist régimes outside Africa. They regard themselves as the founding members of a new third group, the African ex-Colonial International; "People of the Colonies Unite," Kwame Nkrumah wrote in one of his articles. . . .

What can be stated now with near certainty is that, though strongly influenced by some tenets of Soviet ideology, Afro-Communism is showing marked political independence. This does not make it more friendly toward the West. But it is not willing to take orders from the East either; its apparent ambition is to emerge as an independent factor in world politics. . . .

There are other dividing lines between orthodox Leninists and the Afro-Communists. Many of the latter hold strong opinions about the central role of the African intellectuals as the pioneers and leaders of the national liberation movement; the orthodox Communists, on the other hand, disparage the role of the intelligentsia. But the central issue on which opinions widely diverge is the question of the specific character of Africa. The Leninists do not deny the existence of peculiarities in the historical development and present state of Africa, but they maintain that all the basic tenets of Marxism-Leninism are applicable in Africa and that to disregard them would lead to dangerous nationalist deviations. The Afro-Communists, on the other hand, are much more selective in their approval of Leninist theory; while borrowing with much enthusiasm some of the tenets of this body of doctrine, they have emphatically rejected others. Some of their more sophisticated spokesmen who have read the young Marx consider Communism in Europe the natural reaction against a society in which the individual has been alienated; in which money is the supreme good, and in which spiritual values count for little if anything. Africa, in their view, is different; it may be economically backward but it is not a society with its values in process of disintegration; it still has a human richness, warmth and spontaneity sadly lacking in both West and East. These convictions are shared by a majority of African intellectuals and incidentally by quite a number of White missionaries who have called for the "Bantuization of Christianity." On the cultural level these convictions have given rise to the concept of *négritude;* on the political level they have found their reflection in the movement of Pan-Africanism.

Orthodox Leninists are bound to reject both *négritude* and Pan-Africanism as romantic petty-bourgeois nationalist deviations. They try to do so with the maximum of tact, for they realize clearly that this rejection brings them into conflict with the great majority of African political leaders and intellectuals, who all share these views to some degree. For obvious tactical reasons, the orthodox Communists want to prevent a split with the Afro-Communists, but in the long run they cannot afford to compromise, for without clearly defining their own views they cannot hope to make much headway in the future. They face a dilemma which they probably will not be able to resolve, for the prevailing political climate is overwhelmingly in favor of nationalism and Pan-Africanism. The situation in this respect is not dissimilar to the state of affairs in the Middle East a few years ago. The Arab Communists tried very hard to evade, or at any rate to delay, a head-on clash with Pan-Arabism as represented by President Nasser. It is doubtful whether orthodox African Communists will be more successful in postponing the outbreak of what seems otherwise an inevitable conflict.

IV

SINGLE-PARTY SYSTEMS

A remarkable development in contemporary politics has been the proliferation of single-party systems. The term "single party" at present covers a wide variety of forms. In a broad general classification, there are three major types, the first of which might be called the constitutional, *de facto* one-party system; it is sometimes referred to as the "dominant" single-party system. This occurs in a multi-party competitive system where one party is so predominantly successful in open electoral competitions that it exercises power with little threat from other parties. The Congress Party of India in the 1962 elections won 353 seats in the *Lok Sabha* or lower house to 132 seats for all other competing parties. The Party of Revolutionary Institutions (P.R.I.) of Mexico is another dominant party without a serious political rival. This type will not be included in the following discussion since it falls on the democratic rather than dictatorial side because of its competitive basis and its tolerance of an opposition. A second type is the totalitarian one-party system found in communist and fascist states. The outstanding characteristics of this type are the party's total control, elitist membership, suppression of all forms of opposition, and heavy ideological goal orientation. A third type is now appearing with considerable frequency in African and other developing states. It may be described as an authoritarian, at times dictatorial but not totalitarian, single-party system. Within the broad limits of being less competitive than traditional democratic parties but more free than totalitarian, these countries have developed a variety of single-party forms, which are specific adaptations to the particular history and present needs of each. Both authoritarian and totalitarian single parties deny the desirability of competing parties and dislike opposition external to the party. The former, however, may have a mass rather than elite membership; they tend to be more pragmatic than ideological; and they are not totalitarian in scope.

Serious questions arise concerning the nature of totalitarian and authoritarian single-party systems. Can a single party properly be called a party? Are the authoritarian single parties found in some, but not all, emerging states democratic or dictatorial in their orientation? Whether single parties are correctly called "parties" depends, of course, on the concept of a party used as the basis for analysis. Sigmund Neumann, for example, denies that a single party can properly be called a party because he finds that competition with other parties is an essential characteristic.

> Every party in its very essence signifies *partnership* in a particular organization and *separation* from others by a specific program. Such an initial description, to be sure, indicates that the very definition of a party presupposes a democratic climate and hence makes it a misnomer in every dictatorship. A one-party system (*le parti unique*) is a contradiction in itself. Only the co-existence of at least one other competitive group makes a political party real. Still the fact remains that the term has been widely used by modern autocrats, and for a very obvious reason: to keep the semblance of a "people's rule" in their post-democratic dictatorships.[1]

Friedrich and Brzezinski, on the other hand, are more concerned with goals than competition. They are therefore able to define a party in terms that include single-party systems. "A political party is a group of human beings, stably organized with the objective of securing or maintaining for its leaders the control of the government, and with the further objective of giving its members, through such control, ideal and material benefits and advantages." [2] Both sides to the controversy would agree,

---

[1] Sigmund Neumann (ed.), *Modern Political Parties,* University of Chicago Press, 1956, p. 395.
[2] Carl J. Friedrich and Z. K. Brzezinski, *Totalitarian Dictatorship and Autocracy,* Harvard University Press, 1956, p. 28.

however, that totalitarian and authoritarian parties differ significantly from western, democratic competitive parties. Carter and Herz point out some of these differences.

The totalitarian single party is a twentieth-century political phenomenon accompanying the rise of the masses. "Actually, although dictatorship is as old as the hills, dictatorship based on a party, as was the case in Germany and Italy, and as it is today in Soviet Russia and the People's Democracies, is a new kind of political system." [3] As seen above in Lenin's *What Is To Be Done?*, the Communist Party was to act as a conspiratorial vanguard to lead the proletariat into revolution. Once the revolution of 1917 was achieved, Lenin insisted that the party must continue to act as vanguard to carry on the struggle against counter-revolutionaries. Under Stalin the self-perpetuation of the dominant role of the party was continued. He describes the party as the "General Staff" of the proletariat whose function is to organize and control the work of all mass organizations, such as trade unions, and to provide guiding principles for all major decisions. Here Stalin establishes the total power of the party, a position inherent but not explicit in Leninism. Stalin justifies the one-party monopoly on a class basis. Since parties represent classes, any non-proletarian party must necessarily be an enemy of the majority of the people. When a classless society is attained, the inter-party or inter-class struggle ends and the communist party now acts for the whole people. McCloskey and Turner, in the selection given in this chapter, discuss the functions of the party and indicate its relation to the ruling oligarchy.

It is true that in the People's Republic of China and some of the eastern European satellite countries a pseudo-multi-party system exists. In China there are other parties such as the Kuomintang Revolutionary Committee, China Democratic League and the like, whose members have even held office in the governmental structure. However, they do not compete for power and serve rather as a façade for the monopoly of power held by the Communist Party. Mao Tse-tung in adapting Marx-Leninism to

[3] Maurice Duverger, *Political Parties, Their Organization and Activity in the Modern State,* trans. by Barbara and Robert North, Wiley, 1954, p. 255.

Chinese conditions found it necessary to make use of the managerial and other skills of the bourgeoisie and intelligentsia. Accordingly, he established the New Democracy based on a four-class alliance of worker, peasant, petty bourgeoisie and national bourgeoisie, and to maintain this concept, bourgeois parties were retained to symbolize the united front. Li Wei-han, the Director of the United Front Work of the Central Committee of the Communist Party, makes it clear that non-communist parties are to subordinate their activities to communist directives and must ultimately accept thought reform and social transformation. The spurious nature of these minor parties was indicated in their adoption in 1958 of a "charter for the socialist re-modeling of the democratic parties and non-party democrats," which stated as their goals:

> To reform their political standpoint, devotedly and resolutely taking the path of socialism under the leadership of the Communist Party; to be loyal to the socialist system, faithfully carrying out the state's policies and laws, and wholeheartedly contributing their knowledge and strength to the nation's construction; to study from the workers and peasants through practical work, establishing a proper attitude toward physical labor and actively developing the ideology and sentiments possessed by the working people; to study Marx-Leninism and the advanced experience and technique of the Soviet Union; . . .[4]

The authoritarian single parties found in many emerging countries, particularly in Africa, continue the question of whether single parties are "true" parties. Unlike totalitarian single parties, however, they raise the additional question of whether their orientation is democratic or dictatorial. Terms such as "democratic dictatorship" or Sukarno's "guided democracy" may be taken as contradictions in terms or, as the leaders themselves use the terms, as new and necessary forms of political organization. The precise degree of authoritarianism in any particular state is difficult to evaluate because the political institutions themselves are still fluid, changing, and not

---

[4] Quoted in Harold C. Hinton, "The 'Democratic Parties': End of an Experiment?," *Problems of Communism*, No. 3, Vol. VII, May-June 1958, p. 46.

yet in final form. Nor is it possible to generalize accurately
because of the wide variation in forms, each form being
an adaptation of the particular historical and cultural
needs of each state, as Wallerstein points out. However,
a widespread characteristic is a rejection of the western-
type multi-party system as unsuitable for their present
goals of establishing national unity and rapid modernization. Competition among several parties may be rejected
as conducive to corruption, or as divisive in an already
fragile situation, or as a luxury which cannot be afforded
at a time when massive singleness of purpose and solidarity of effort are needed to achieve social and economic
change. The alternative forms chosen vary widely. Sukarno, distrusting both liberal democracy and its multi-
party system, did not establish a single party as such but
approached the same end by permitting only certain
compliant parties to exist and emasculating them by regulations laid down in the name of his "guided democracy."
Sékou Touré of Guinea established a single mass (but not
class) party, which is structured along communist party
lines of democratic centralism with 2,885 party branches,
a membership of 1,600,000 in a population of 3,000,000,
and buttressed with mass youth and women's organizations. The official chart indicates the primacy of party
over government. Nasser, on the other hand, outlawed all
parties because he was disgusted with the corruption and
self-interest of the traditional Egyptian parties and felt the
need for a patriotic dedication of all the people rather
than loyalty to a particular class or party. In place of
parties he substituted a single, all-embracing "movement"
called since 1962 the Arab Socialist Union. Horton discusses the difficulty which Nasser, as well as leaders elsewhere, finds in creating a sense of national unity and
national purpose necessary for effecting social and economic change.

A key to the nature of totalitarian and authoritarian
single-party systems is the attitude toward opposition.
Communist parties reject absolutely all opposition external to the party as contrary to the Marxist laws of social
and political development, as Stalin baldly states. While
positing theoretically the principle of "democratic centralism" within the party whereby there is freedom of discus-

sion prior to a decision but disciplined adherence there-after, in practice there is discussion at most only within the confines of a policy proposed by the top party elite. Mao Tse-tung's position is formulated more subtly, but it is basically the same. He says that there are two types of contradiction, those between the people and their enemies and those among the people. The former is antagonistic and must be suppressed, but the latter, if properly handled, can be resolved in a peaceful way. However, it is the party that determines which contradictions are antagonistic, that is, who are enemies of the people.

In emerging countries, attitudes toward the opposition show considerable variation, but on the whole opposition is considered undesirable. Sukarno simply bans those parties which oppose him as counter-revolutionaries working for the downfall of the state. However, the more usual basis of objection to opposition is that contests between opposing forces are a waste of time and energy. "There is no opposition for opposition's sake and no struggle by individuals to take over power from other individuals in Guinea. Such struggles are a waste of time and energy and therefore inefficient in new countries where social programs are the first consideration." [5] Nyerere of Tanganyika agrees that opposition between parties is an unwarranted dissipation of national energy, however essential it may seem to western democratic countries, but he insists that there is ample room for the free, democratic procedure of discussion within the party. The final issue rests on whether indeed there is freedom within the single party or movement or whether freedom to oppose *within* the party is also eroded and limited in the name of efficiency.

[5] Abdoulaye Diallo. Quoted in George W. Shepherd, Jr., *The Politics of African Nationalism,* 1962, Frederick A. Praeger, Inc., p. 99.

A. THE NATURE OF SINGLE PARTIES

— 1 —

GOVERNMENT AND POLITICS IN THE TWENTIETH CENTURY

Gwendolen M. Carter and John Herz[*]

The simplest of all modern political forms is the one-party dictatorship. Its concentration of political authority in the hands of the executive and administration is under-pinned by the all-pervasive influence of a highly organized political party which can scarcely be differentiated from the governmental machinery which it operates. Though representative organs are commonly a part of the structure of modern one-party dictatorships, it is not their purpose to provide control, but rather to serve as a sounding board for political pronouncements. Law and the courts do not operate as separate independent entities authorized to decide disputes concerning the operations of other governmental organs, but act to reinforce the norms of behavior laid down by the party leadership and ratified by the executive and administration. This remains true even when these norms are radically changed in response to new objectives. Thus, it is characteristic of one-party dictatorships that all the organs of government—executive, administrative, legislative and judicial —find their overriding purpose in the objectives of the

* Gwendolen M. Carter and John H. Herz, *Government and Politics in the Twentieth Century,* 1961, Frederick A. Praeger, Inc., pp. 22-24, 100-101, 114-118. Reprinted by permission.

regime, and that these objectives are formulated by the leaders of the one political party which infiltrates and directs not only political, but also economic, social, and, in principle, even highly personal affairs.

Having said this, however, it is necessary to point out that within this over-all definition of the one-party dictatorship, there is a wide variety in the ways in which its instrumentalities are used and the purposes to which they are directed. Fascist states, like Hitler's Germany and, though somewhat less so, Mussolini's Italy, were molded by particular appeals (Hitler to "blood and soil," Mussolini to the glories of ancient Rome) which tended to make them *sui generis,* while Communism has certain universal tenets and notions of historical evolution which provide a compulsion toward unity and uniformity among Communist states. However, despite this compulsion toward a general unity, there is increasing evidence of variety among the Communist states themselves, with Poland, for example, tending to modify dictatorial practices and slowing down the processes of social and economic change, while China presses ahead the socialization of agriculture and village life and the "communization" of all life with a rapidity and ruthlessness greater even than that used in the early days of the Five-Year Plans of the Soviet Union. Within the Soviet Union itself, which has had by far the longest history of any of the modern one-party dictatorships, it is now possible to identify three eras: the revolutionary mass-party movement of Lenin, organized and carried through under disciplined leadership, but still retaining its appeal for popular support; the strongly statist regime of Stalin, in which centralized authority backed by brutality and frequent purges forced a social and economic revolution in order to create a powerful industrial structure; and the Khrushchev era, with its greater flexibility combined with increased party control operating through local as well as central organs.

Nonetheless, despite great differences in their use of power and even in the allocation of authority, there is relatively little variation among the one-party dictatorships in the political form itself. The key remains the concentration of power in a single party whose influence permeates every aspect of life and which provides the most powerful means of centralized and all-pervasive rule which has yet been developed. . . .

Dictatorships also find the political party an indispensable instrument, but they use it in a very different way than do democracies. Where democratic political parties consciously emphasize diversity and mutual criticism, the political party in the Communist or Fascist dictatorship is the body of the faithful who are dedicated to maintaining the one truth which their leaders avow. Whereas, apart from their elected members, democratic political parties are informal, nongovernmental organizations (though particularly in the United States their activities must be carried on within a network of governmental regulations), the dictatorial political party permeates every governmental as well as nongovernmental activity and is virtually indistinguishable, except in name, from the administration which it dominates. Where democratic systems maximize opportunities for criticism and protect individual rights to free speech, dictatorial systems operate on the principle of "democratic centralism," i.e., that comments may be offered only in the early stages of a proposal, but once the leaders have made their decision everyone must accept it. Where democracies anticipate an alternation of leaders and provide the public with a choice of candidates for office, dictatorial leaders are self-selected through a power struggle within the party machinery itself. Where democracies use the fervor and slogans of an electoral campaign to publicize the differences between party programs, the party in a dictatorial state carries on continual propaganda campaigns in support of the government's objectives and is the chief means by which conformity is maintained throughout the society.

It is thus confusing and, in a sense, inappropriate to use the term "political party" not only for the competing political associations in democratic states but also for that group which has the full monopoly of political as well as of all other powers in a dictatorial totalitarian state. A prime characteristic of political parties as they have evolved in democratic countries is that they are voluntary groupings which acquire their cohesion from perceived and accepted purposes. Democratic political parties also socially integrate the people within their ranks by giving them a common objective and a common organization. But the political party in such states is a vehicle to be used by its members, not a master to give them orders. In totalitarian states, in contrast, the political party is the chief means of control throughout the state, and thus its membership is carefully sifted to ensure conformity to the overriding purpose of the small governing group. To a certain degree the political party serves the purpose of expressing the sentiments of its members, but only to the degree that is useful for the purposes of the regime. In no case does it act to restrain the exercise of power. As the Nazis used to put it: in democracies authority comes from below and responsibility from above; in dictatorships authority comes from above and responsibility from below. . . .

While mass parties evolved slowly in the older democratic states, they have been a characteristic of the newer states from the beginning. Where a nationalistic movement is struggling to bring a country to independence, its natural focus is in a mass party which unites virtually all elements in the country in a common demand for transfer of power. As independence comes close or is achieved, strains may develop, however, which split the mass party into communal or tribally oriented groups. In British India, for example, the Moslem League refused to work with the Congress Party with its largely Hindu support and secular philosophy, and the ultimate result was that the subcontinent had to be partitioned between Pakistan and India.

In the Republic of India, the Congress Party has managed to maintain its dominant position despite challenges from both the socialist parties on the left and the communal parties on the right, but largely because of the personal magnetism of Pandit Nehru rather than because of its own vigor. In Pakistan, the Moslem League split badly after losing its best leaders through death or assassination, and the country is now under army rule.

In the Gold Coast (subsequently Ghana), middle-class and tribally oriented groups combined against the standard-bearer of nationalism, Kwame Nkrumah's Convention Peoples Party (commonly known as the CPP), in the years immediately preceding independence. In an effort to satisfy them, the British insisted that Ghana should establish regional assemblies to share power with the national legislature, but these were voted out of existence almost as soon as they came into being; moreover, the opposition has steadily diminished in strength, due partly to governmental arbitrariness, partly to its own policy and tactical mistakes, and partly to the difficulty of retaining support without being able to provide the kind of benefits which government can bestow. Rapid and impressive development plans have done much to unify Ghana but also further to strengthen Nkrumah's government, and it seems unlikely that the opposition will be able in the foreseeable future to challenge its power.

Is there then no middle way between a dominant mass party in newly developing states and anarchy threatening to lead to army or dictatorial rule? Possibly not. The problem of emerging Asian and African states still is more social than political: It is the need to build a strong enough sense of unity in the country so that criticism and diversity do not appear to be treason. Wherever there is a serious split in the nationalist movement prior to independence, the group which stands in opposition is almost inevitably labeled treasonable. If this split persists after independence, either force or a long period of stability are needed to heal it. The kind of divisions which are welcomed in well-established democracies may shatter the fragile chances of national unity in tribally oriented societies.

In Tanganyika, most promising of the multiracial states (its small percentage of white persons and the somewhat larger Asian component support the African nationalist movement), Julius Nyerere, founder and leader of the Tanganyika African National Union, which is progressively taking over political responsibilities as the country moves steadily toward independence, speaks eloquently of "one-party democracy." Nyerere's view is that everyone must combine within the mass party which is leading the country to self-rule and that this same mass party will inevitably conduct the government after independence has been won. He refuses to acknowledge the right to criticism of anyone not within this movement. At the same time, he asserts that anyone who does dedicate himself to the progress of independence is justified in criticizing the actions of the governing group and even in establishing an alternative political party if the nationalist standard-bearer should fail in its tasks of building social solidarity and stimulating economic growth. The difference between this contention and developments in Ghana is that in Tanganyika opposition must arise from *within* the nationalistic group to be recognized as legitimate.

Is this democracy? We have been accustomed to say that one-party rule and dictatorship were virtually synonymous. But even in the early days of the United States, there was only one party, the Federalists, until Jefferson stimulated the rise of what was little more than a personal political movement. When the Federalist Party collapsed, the country was left for some time without an organized alternative to Jefferson's Republican Party. Yet in the long run, of course, the American two-party system emerged. While it is natural for the older Western democracies to look for two-party systems and ultimate alternation of office in the new countries, these require experience, a substantial pool of talent, and a fairly firm social structure. It has developed, and may well last, in Nigeria, where the very diversity of the three regions encourages such a process. But for most of the new countries, the touchstone of democracy will be the right to express open criticism and the maintenance of the rule of law. If these two essentials exist, the future may well see the evolution of what we consider the more orthodox structure of democratic government.

What we have called "one-party democracy" differs basically, it must be emphasized, from the one-party totalitarianism of the Soviet Union itself or other Communist-controlled countries. To have only one party in the first instance is not a dogma but an expedient. The objective is to mobilize the people voluntarily to work for the vastly important objective of national development. In this sense, "one-party democracy" parallels the unity most Western democratic states established while they were fighting what President Franklin D. Roosevelt called "the war of survival"—World War II. In contrast, the "peoples' democracies" accept one-party rule as permanent, stamp out opposition, and regard the party as the agent to secure conformism. Thus, despite occasional relaxations, they are far closer to Soviet totalitarianism than to Nyerere's "one-party democracy."

The possibilities of criticism within the one-party democracy provide in themselves a type of opposition which should not be underestimated. The mass parties in the newly developing countries are far from monolithic. It is far more difficult to identify and classify the kind of opposition which operates, for example, within Felix Houphouet-Boigny's RDA (*Rassemblement Démocratique Africain*), which holds all the seats in the Ivory Coast, than it would be if the opposition were organized as a separate party—but its existence has been abundantly evidenced by changing policies. In other words, something very close to the interplay of government and opposition in mature democracies may take place within the one party of the new states, but only, of course, if opportunities for criticism are not stifled.

B. THE TOTALITARIAN SINGLE-PARTY SYSTEM

— 1 —

PROBLEMS OF LENINISM
Joseph Stalin*

This new party is the party of Leninism.
What are the specific features of this new party?

* Joseph Stalin, *Problems of Leninism*, 1954, Foreign Languages Publishing House, Moscow, pp. 96-98, 166-167, 170, 699-700.

1) *The Party as the advanced detachment of the working class*. The Party must be, first of all, the *advanced* detachment of the working class. The Party must absorb all the best elements of the working class, their experience, their revolutionary spirit, their selfless devotion to the cause of the proletariat. But in order that it may really be the advanced detachment, the Party must be armed with revolutionary theory, with a knowledge of the laws of the movement, with a knowledge of the laws of revolution. Without this it will be incapable of directing the struggle of the proletariat, of leading the proletariat. The Party cannot be a real party if it limits itself to registering what the masses of the working class feel and think, if it drags at the tail of the spontaneous movement, if it is unable to overcome the inertia and the political indifference of the spontaneous movement, if it is unable to rise above the momentary interests of the proletariat, if it is unable to raise the masses to the level of understanding the class interests of the proletariat. The Party must stand at the head of the working class; it must see further than the working class; it must lead the proletariat, and not drag at the tail of the spontaneous movement. . . .

The Party is the political leader of the working class.

I have already spoken of the difficulties of the struggle of the working class, of the complicated conditions of the struggle, of strategy and tactics, of reserves and manoeuvering, of attack and retreat. These conditions are no less complicated, if not more so, than the conditions of war. Who can see clearly in these conditions, who can give correct guidance to the proletarian millions? No army at war can dispense with an experienced General Staff if it does not want to be doomed to defeat. Is it not clear that the proletariat can still less dispense with such a General Staff if it does not want to allow itself to be devoured by its mortal enemies? But where is this General Staff? Only the revolutionary party of the proletariat can serve as this General Staff. The working class without a revolutionary party is an army without a General Staff.

The Party is the General Staff of the proletariat.

But the Party cannot be only an *advanced* detachment.

It must at the same time be a detachment of the *class,* part of the class, closely bound up with it by all the fibres of its being. The distinction between the advanced detachment and the rest of the working class, between Party members and non-Party people, cannot disappear until classes disappear; it will exist as long as the ranks of the proletariat continue to be replenished with former members of other classes, as long as the working class as a whole is not in a position to rise to the level of the advanced detachment. But the Party would cease to be a party if this distinction developed into a gap, if the Party turned in on itself and became divorced from the non-Party masses. The Party cannot lead the class if it is not connected with the non-Party masses, if there is no bond between the Party and the non-Party masses, if these masses do not accept its leadership, if the Party enjoys no moral and political credit among the masses. . . .

Its strength lies in the fact that it draws into its ranks all the best elements of the proletariat from all the mass organizations of the latter. Its function is to *combine* the work of all the mass organizations of the proletariat without exception and to *direct* their activities towards a single goal, the goal of the emancipation of the proletariat. And it is absolutely necessary to combine and direct them towards a single goal, for otherwise unity in the struggle of the proletariat is impossible, for otherwise the guidance of the proletarian masses in their struggle for power, in their struggle for building socialism, is impossible. But only the vanguard of the proletariat, its Party, is capable of combining and directing the work of the mass organizations of the proletariat. Only the party of the proletariat, only the Communist Party, is capable of fulfilling this role of main leader in the system of the dictatorship of the proletariat. . . .

Not a single important decision is arrived at by the mass organizations of the proletariat without guiding directives from the Party. That is perfectly true. But does that mean that the dictatorship of the proletariat *consists entirely* of the guiding directives given by the Party? Does that mean that, in view of this, the guiding directives of the Party can be identified with the dictatorship of the proletariat? Of course not. The dictatorship of the proletariat consists of the guiding directives of the Party plus the carrying out of these directives by the mass organizations of the proletariat, plus their fulfilment by the population. . . .

As to freedom for various political parties, we adhere to somewhat different views. A party is a part of a class, its most advanced part. Several parties, and, consequently, freedom for parties, can exist only in a society in which there are antagonistic classes whose interests are mutually hostile and irreconcilable—in which there are, say, capitalists and workers, landlords and peasants, kulaks and poor peasants, etc. But in the U.S.S.R. there are no longer such classes as the capitalists, the landlords, the kulaks, etc. In the U.S.S.R. there are only two classes, workers and peasants, whose interests—far from being mutually hostile—are, on the contrary, friendly. Hence, there is no ground in the U.S.S.R. for the existence of several parties, and, consequently, for freedom for these parties. In the U.S.S.R. there is ground only for one party, the Communist Party. In the U.S.S.R. only one party can exist, the Communist Party, which courageously defends the interests of the workers and peasants to the very end. And that it defends the interests of these classes not at all badly, of that there can hardly be any doubt. (*Loud applause.*)

They talk of democracy. But what is democracy? Democracy in capitalist countries, where there are antagonistic classes, is, in the last analysis, democracy for the strong, democracy for the propertied minority. In the U.S.S.R., on the contrary, democracy is democracy for the working people, i.e., democracy for all.

— 2 —

THE SOVIET DICTATORSHIP
Herbert McClosky
and John E. Turner*

However lofty the position of the Communist Party in official theory, its place in the Soviet system can best be understood by reference to its actual role as the servant of the dictatorship. Although the dictatorship rests principally upon the Party, the Party in turn is subservient to an oligarchy of Communist leaders who exploit the organization as their most reliable arm. Since the oligarchy has vast, almost unlimited powers, the functions performed by the Party in its behalf are necessarily very broad. In general, these functions can be classified as follows.

1. The Communist Party makes available to Soviet leaders a large, highly organized, and carefully screened group of supporters, many of whom are zealous and/or ambitious Communists, eager to do whatever the dictatorship requires of them. This huge reservoir of talent is strategically placed to dominate all the social formations of Soviet life. The Party's elaborate machinery is also geared to select thousands of reliable non-Party people who help in the conduct of public affairs. According to an official source, the Party "concentrates in its hands the selection and allocation of cadres. . . . It places in leading posts of the government, the economy, the cooperatives, and other institutions those people who understand the meaning and significance of Party directives. . . ."

* From *The Soviet Dictatorship* by McClosky and Turner, pp. 200-202. Copyright, 1960, McGraw-Hill Book Company, Inc. Used by permission.

The Party is thus a recruitment agency for the Soviet elite and a "school" for training Communist leaders.

2. The Party serves as the repository and guardian of official ideology. Unlike free states, the Soviet dictatorship permits expression only of beliefs approved by the oligarchy. Once the leaders have "interpreted" the sacred teachings and issued "important directives and instructions" for their enforcement, the Party acts as the principal carrier of these beliefs. Communist officials boast that the Party has been trained "to display stern Bolshevik intolerance towards all sorts of deviations. . . ." The Party thus takes on the characteristics of an invisible church, helping to enforce the "true" doctrine as ordained by its leaders. Through its network of propaganda outlets, it attempts to indoctrinate the masses with "correct" views and to inspire them to support the official line. It guides the state in "educating" the Soviet people: "Under the leadership of the Communist Party . . . the Soviet state directs the spiritual life of the society and secures, in this way, its successful advancement to the higher communist forms of life. . . ."

3. As the central thread of the totalitarian complex, the Party holds together the confused network of political, economic, and social institutions in the U.S.S.R., coordinating their activities. It supervises the national effort to achieve the political and economic goals of the dictatorship. A decision reached in the Party Presidium is transmitted to all levels of the Communist apparatus and relayed to the government agencies, the economic enterprises, and the mass organizations, which are themselves staffed by Communists. The job of the Party is to "unify" and provide direction "for the whole complex system of state organs and mass organizations, concentrating all of the energies of the Soviet people on the tasks of . . . building the communist society."

4. The Party also assumes major responsibility for seeing that the oligarchy's decisions are carried out. "It is not enough for a Party member merely to agree with Party decisions; it is incumbent upon him to strive actively to have them put into effect." To this end the regime places Party units and individual Communists in every type of Soviet establishment (factories, govern-

ment ministries, collective farms, military groups, cultural centers, and educational and research institutions). Party members are expected to serve as watchdogs for the dictatorship, reporting breaches of labor discipline, corruption, and other violations. They are also expected to function as agitators and propagandists, inspiring Soviet citizens to devote themselves to the fulfillment of the regime's directives. The 8 million members of the Communist Party thus afford the dictatorship an army of agents who are stationed at every key point of Soviet society in an effort to control it totally.

5. The Party is, finally, the vital link between the dictatorship and the masses, the chief instrument for inspiring and organizing mass participation and for engineering mass consent. It is mainly the Party that supplies the mass meetings, the demonstrations, the staged elections, the "socialist competitions," the agitational slogans, and the innumerable propaganda campaigns, by which modern dictatorships seek to rally popular support and to give the appearance of being "democratic." Official sources repeatedly claim that the Soviet state "does not stand above the masses, is not divorced from, but, on the contrary, merges with them . . . (drawing them) into the everyday work of managing the state. In the Soviet country millions of workers and peasants have been given the opportunity of taking part in the administration of the state, and of unfolding their creative faculties and organizing abilities. . . . (This) development of socialist democracy . . . led by the Party . . . reinforces the strength and might of the state and accelerates the onward march of the Soviet people towards communism." The Party holds together and coordinates the "entire system of mass state and public organizations," the so-called "transmission belts" and "levers" which connect the masses with the dictatorship.

— 3 —

THE CHINESE PEOPLE'S DEMOCRATIC UNITED FRONT
Li Wei-han*

It was through the steeling of dozens of years of revolutionary war that the great, glorious and correct Communist Party, the broad united front and the powerful Peoples Liberation Army—both led by the Communist Party—were born. It was by relying on these three magic weapons and through the peasant revolutionary war and the revolutionary base areas in the countryside, that the powerful state of the people's democratic dictatorship (in essence, the proletarian dictatorship) was established. The people's democratic dictatorship is the crystallization and the concentrated expression of these three magic weapons, which ensured that China should make the transition to socialism by peaceful means. After the founding of the People's Republic of China, the people's democratic united front has changed from a united front with the armed struggle as its mainstay to a united front with the dictatorship of the proletariat as its basis, a united front for carrying out peaceful transformation and peaceful construction.

The people's democratic dictatorship in China is in essence a proletarian dictatorship. The objectives and functions of this dictatorship are: to suppress within the country the reactionary classes, cliques and exploiters who resist the socialist revolution; to guard against subversive enemy activities and possible aggression from abroad; to eliminate completely the exploitation of man

* Li Wei-han, "The Chinese People's Democratic United Front," *Peking Review*, No. 34, August 25, 1961, p. 18.

by man; to transform the whole of society according to socialist principles; to build our country into a socialist state with a modern industry, a modern agriculture, and a modern science and culture, and then gradually effect the transition to communism. ". . . the dictatorship of the proletariat requires not only that the proletariat should exercise strong leadership over the state organs, but also that the broadest masses of the people should participate actively in the state organs. Neither of these can be dispensed with." Our Party long ago pointed out that the broad united front which is led by the working class and embraces various nationalities, democratic classes, democratic parties and people's organizations, is necessary not only for the people's democratic revolution, but also for the realization of the socialist cause.

Some think that the united front is unnecessary if we want to carry on the proletarian dictatorship and build socialism. They don't understand that we have had a long history of maintaining a united front with the national bourgeoisie, the democratic parties and other patriots. In the socialist stage, despite their negative side of trying to take the capitalist road, the national bourgeoisie are willing to remain in the united front and accept socialist transformation. Therefore, we have no reason not to continue to co-operate with them. Besides, the national bourgeoisie is a class which possesses relatively rich knowledge and culture and a relatively large number of intellectuals and specialists. The working class should continue to maintain the united front with the national bourgeoisie, because the united front will play an important role in educating and reforming them and because their knowledge can be made use of to serve socialism, while the enemy can be isolated to the maximum and the anti-imperialist forces can be strengthened. Those who think that the proletarian dictatorship needs no united front know still less about this: ". . . we have no reason not to adopt the policy of long-term co-existence with all other democratic parties which are truly devoted to the task of uniting the people for the cause of socialism and which enjoy the trust of the people." It is quite obvious that the united front led by the working class and based on the worker-peasant alliance will not only do no damage to the proletarian dictatorship, but, on the contrary, will help it consolidate itself and grow.

Some hold that since the working class wants to continue to maintain united-front relations with the national bourgeoisie in the socialist stage, the proletarian dictatorship should be weakened or even abandoned. In 1957 the bourgeois rightists clamoured that they wanted no Party leadership and no proletarian dictatorship. The experience gained after liberation proves that it is only under the conditions of the proletarian dictatorship and it is only when the working class through its vanguard the Communist Party exercises leadership over the state political power and the broad masses of the people, that the task of the socialist revolution can be thoroughly accomplished. It is only with the weapon of the proletarian dictatorship which the working class wields through its vanguard the Communist Party that all those who are willing to take the socialist road can be rallied around itself for the joint execution of the political line of the working class.

C. AUTHORITARIAN SINGLE-PARTY SYSTEMS IN DEVELOPING COUNTRIES

— 1 —

AFRICA, THE POLITICS OF INDEPENDENCE

Immanuel Wallerstein*

We speak of *the party*, but are there not *parties?* There are in some countries. Most African nations came to

* From *Africa, The Politics of Independence* by Immanuel

independence by organizing a nationalist movement which laid effective claim to power. The standard pattern was the existence of one major party which symbolized the struggle for independence, with some weak, often regionalist, opposition parties. Ghana, Togo, Sierra Leone, Somalia are examples of this. In some few cases, as a result of either absorption or suppression, the opposition totally ceased to exist before independence—notably in the Ivory Coast, the Republic of Mali, Tunisia; or it expired soon after independence—as in Guinea and Upper Volta. Where there was no one party which commanded overwhelming support—the Congo, Sudan, Nigeria—or where the nationalist party split after independence, as in Morocco, there often was considerable trouble. Where a major segment of the nationalist movement was systematically excluded from power, as in Cameroun, there was continued civil war. Almost everywhere, the trend after independence has been in one of two directions: toward a one-party state with consequent stability (if the resulting single party grouped the major elements) or toward a breakdown of the party system with consequent instability and a tendency for the army to play a growing role (Sudan, Morocco, Congo).

The choice has not been between one-party and multiparty states; it has been between one-party states and either anarchy or military regimes or various combinations of the two. The military regime, beset by internal trouble, finds it difficult to mobilize energies for economic development, to keep the intellectuals satisfied and in line, to allow for participation in government by any factions other than the small ruling group. On the contrary, the single-party state—at least the single-party state where the party structure is well articulated and really functioning—provides a mechanism whereby the majority of the population can have some regular, meaningful connection with, and influence upon, the governmental process, and vice versa.

Since "single-party systems" seem to be a standard feature of the new African nations, it is well to distin-

Wallerstein, 1961, Random House, pp. 95-99, 163-165. Reprinted by permission.

guish them from the "single-party systems" in Eastern
Europe, for example. The party in Africa, heir of the
nationalist movement, is first of all a mass party, at least
in theory. It seeks to enroll all the citizenry in its branches,
including its women's and youth sections. In those nations
where the party is an effective and real one, the sections
meet on a regular basis, often weekly, in every village
and town ward. Because almost the whole population
belongs to the party, these meetings resemble "town meetings." The function of the meetings is twofold. They are
arenas whereby the government via the party cadres can
transmit new ideas, new projects, new demands for
sacrifices—that is, they function to educate the population, so that government decisions do not remain dead
letters but are really carried out. But they also serve to
communicate the ideas of the people to the government
as well; they are a direct channel of complaint and suggestion through which the government can be made sensitive to the internal realities of the nation and flexible
in the means it uses to achieve its goals. There seems to
be considerable evidence that this two-way process is not
a sham, or in any sense based on terror, but that it works
fairly well. Of course it works better in some places than
in others. Tunisia, Mali, Guinea, Tanganyika are models
of single-party states with two-way communication.
Ghana, Togo and the Central African Republic run close
behind. Some party structures place less emphasis on
participation, using more nebulous antennae to remain
sensitive to popular will. In these cases, the pipe lines
transmitting points of view—both upward and downward
—sometimes get clogged. The Ivory Coast is a prime
example of this, and Ivory Coast leaders often discuss
the need to revitalize the party structure in order to bring
it into line with parties of other countries providing more
active communication.

Along with such a structure goes an ideology which
argues that the party incarnates the nation, not because
it is in tune with historical destiny, but because of its
past and present accomplishments. In the past, it fought
for freedom and helped to create a national consciousness. And in the present, it is a mass, not a class, party.
If it is not a class party, it is even less an elite party.

(This is, of course, a fundamental theoretical difference between African parties and Communist parties in Eastern Europe.) It is a party to which everyone is encouraged to adhere, and to which the majority do adhere.

This ideology is the basis of justification for the theory of parallel authority—the matching of each governmental structure (national, regional, local) with a party structure, priority always being assigned to the political over the administrative structure. It is considered the essence of popular control over government in Ghana and the Ivory Coast, Niger and Tanganyika, that the Political Bureau of the party should take precedence over the Cabinet. The party should run the government, not vice versa, because the party, not the government, is the emanation of the people, that is, holds their loyalty and ties them to the state. The party integrates the nation and allows the integration to be accomplished by a method that maximizes the opportunity of every citizen to participate on a regular and meaningful basis in the decision-making process. In practice small elites may still run the show, but they do so to a lesser degree than if there were no party structure.

The party is not alone, however, in performing the integrating function. It shares the stage with its most important adjunct, the national hero. The hero, the leader, is not an isolated phenomenon. He is the leader of the party as well as of the nation. Should he break his ties with the party, he could find it difficult to survive, as we see from the decline of Messali Hadj in Algeria. Nevertheless, his power is not identical with that of the party; he has a drawing power of his own, as a potential arbiter, as a militant fighter, as one who has proved his mettle and will seek the nation's good.

The appearance of national heroes in Africa often makes outside observers uncomfortable, for the latter think of parallel strong men and "dictators" elsewhere. It is important, therefore, to see why the hero looms so large in the new African nations and what function he really fulfills.

Not all "heroes" are alike. Bourguiba of Tunisia and Nkrumah of Ghana, even Abbé Fulbert Youlou in the Congo (Brazzaville) represent one style—flamboyant, triumphant, evangelizing. Sékou Touré of Guinea, Modibo Keita of Mali, even Azikiwe of Nigeria, perhaps Nyerere of Tanganyika represent another style—calculating, militant, analytical. Olympio of Togo, Houphouet-Boigny of the Ivory Coast, even Senghor of Senegal and Ferhat Abbas of Algeria represent a third style—more cautious, sure-footed, quiet. These styles may make a lot of difference in the history of pan-Africanism. They make less difference internally. The functions of the hero at home are everywhere substantially the same. The methods employed are similar.

The role of the hero is first of all to be a readily available, easily understood, symbol of the new nation, someone to incarnate in his person its values and aspirations. But the hero does more than symbolize the new nation. He legitimizes the state by ordaining obedience to its norms out of loyalty to his person. This is what people usually mean when they speak of the charismatic authority of these leaders. . . .

The assessment of the degree of democracy in African states must be based on an appreciation of the alternatives that exist. The choice is not between a one-party system and a multi-party parliamentary system. The structural prerequisites for the latter do not yet exist to a sufficient degree in Africa. The effective choice for the newly independent states is between a one-party (or one-dominant-party) system, which allows for some real popular participation in, and control over, the government, or anarchy, which means that power reverts to local princelings and patrons, remote from the intellectual contact and stimulation which infuses the modernizing elite of the national structures.

The one-party system in the African context is often a significant step toward the liberal state, not a first step away from it. For the purpose of the one-party system is to create a national state sufficiently well-rooted in the loyalties of its citizens so that the distinction between state and government will begin to emerge. Without this basic loyalty, the relative stability of the state cannot be assumed, and governments will continue to refuse to tolerate opposition that is not contained within their own party, for fear that such opposition will lead to the dismantlement of the state. This fear is not wholly without foundation.

The national orientation of the mass of citizens is not the sole prerequisite for the creation of institutions that can guarantee the rights of opposition, even outside the party. African states, as we have seen, are determined to raise their economic level by industrializing and by mechanizing their agriculture. The point of economic development is to achieve greater equality with the rest of the world, as well as to further the integration of the nation. A developed economy creates a new pattern of social strata. Occupational and income groupings become more nearly balanced. The disproportion of a situation where 95 percent of the population are peasant farmers disappears. As this new stratification develops, the interest groupings of citizens become defined largely in terms of these economic and occupational roles. But these groupings tend to be nationwide rather than regional in scope, which the present groupings based on ethnic considerations usually are. As interests become nationwide, opposition will cease to lead to territorial secession, since territorial secession will then usually be irrelevant to the political objectives of the opposition.

Dissent and discussion in African states today are guaranteed in part by African tradition, in part by the continued political turmoil. These are not long-term guarantees, since tradition is being weakened and turmoil may cease. The one-party systems may begin to stagnate without any internal structural protection for the opposition (independent judiciary, free press, etc.). This is clearly a danger of the future. Yet these structural guarantees will not be acceptable as long as they threaten the preservation of the state. The building up of loyalty to the nation, combined with the economic differentiation that development will bring, plus the resulting creation of nationwide interest groups will create a situation in which the institution of structural guarantees will no longer threaten the preservation of the state.

It does not follow, however, that these structural guarantees will thereupon be instituted. The emergence of long-range institutional guarantees of a democratic society is by no means automatic. However, it is not really possible at all before the prerequisites are fulfilled. The problem therefore is twofold: how to fulfill the prerequisites as rapidly as possible, and how to do so in such a way as to maximize the possibility that the authoritarian regimes of the present will not stagnate and harden but will develop further toward the increase of personal freedom within the state.

— 2 —

RES PUBLICA! ONCE MORE RES PUBLICA!
President Sukarno*

First: IN ORDER TO MAKE THE PARTY SYSTEM SOUND, THE POLITICAL PARTIES SHOULD BE SIMPLIFIED AND MADE MORE MODEST. THIS WILL BE REGULATED BY A POLITICAL PARTY LAW AND BY MEANS OF ALTERING AND/OR PERFECTING THE ELECTORAL LAW, THAT IS, LAW NO. 7 OF 1953.
THE POLITICAL PARTIES WILL NOT BE DISSOLVED.

This is a most important question! Over and over again in my earlier speeches I have called for making the political party system sound and healthy in our country, to make the parties in our country more modest, to do away with the multi-party system in Indonesia.

When I say so, it does not mean that I hate the prin-

* President Sukarno, *Res Publica! Once More Res Publica!*
   Ministry of Information, Republic of Indonesia, 1959, pp.
   40-43.

ciple of having political parties, hate their respective
ideologies, hate their leaders.

I still continue to appreciate and respect the great and
small services which have been rendered by those parties
to our Country and Nation, both in the past colonial
period and also in the present period of independence.

I want to eradicate something else. I want to eradicate the difficulties being suffered by our State and Society because of the conditions in our parties in Indonesia.
I want to eradicate the excesses.

In the address I gave when this Constituent Assembly
was inaugurated, amongst other things I warned that the
struggle for power between the parties had already become so acute that in reality it was endangering the State,
so that I was compelled to issue a reminder that: if the
party leaders did not rein themselves in, did not set
bounds upon themselves, did not exercise self-discipline,
it was certain that a revolutionary situation would break
out explosively and that its tumult would very likely
sweep aside those leaders themselves.

Then in constructing my concept, that so well-known
concept designed *to make* the Republic of Indonesia *safe,*
which I made public on 21 February 1957, I again very
clearly criticised the party system in Indonesia, especially
the system of "opposition" which felt it had no responsibility for saying that the Government did good things,
the opposition which felt it its duty always to criticise
the Government as severely as possible and *"coûte que
coûte"*—the opposition which was always trying to overthrow the Government in order to exchange it for a
Government formed of the opposition itself.

All the difficulties and excesses which arise out of the
party system in Indonesia, especially out of the multi-
party system, are the consequences of the prevalence of
the principle of liberal democracy in our country, which
in another part of this address I have indicated as being
unsuited to the climate of Indonesia.

In the sphere of Guided Democracy which—God
willing—we shall enter soon when we return to the 1945
Constitution, it would be difficult to continue political
party practices as we have known them up to now.

How shall we go about making them sound?

The Government does not intend to abolish the parties. But the Government considers it necessary to make the situation in our political parties suited to the atmosphere of Guided Democracy.

The Government will propose a *Draft Political Party Law* in order to make the conditions of our parties *more modest* in the sense of *reducing the number of parties;* this effort to make party conditions sound can also be implemented through the Law perfecting Law No. 7 of 1953 (the Electoral Law). That draft is also being prepared.

The Fundamentals of that effort are:

1. To make orderly and to regulate, in line with what is proper, the life of the parties as an instrument of struggle and of implementation of the ideals of the Indonesian Nation, as laid down in the 1945 Constitution:

2. To fix the norms and the ethical code of the parties, which shall be aimed in the first place at the safety of the State and the people of Indonesia, and meanwhile to fix the bounds of party work, for example, the bounds of the safety of the State, the bounds of the interests of the majority of the people, the bounds of the National identity, the bounds of morality and the bounds of responsibility to God. Apart from this, conditions will also be set concerning their statutes, their guides to work.

3. To make new stipulations for when a party may participate in the right to be elected.

In these efforts to make the parties sound, of course there will be a thorough review made of the Government Decree of the Republic of Indonesia dated 3 November 1945, which concerns the political parties.

By these efforts, the Government hopes to be able to eliminate or at least to lessen, the excesses and difficulties arising from the party system, especially the multiparty system, in Indonesia, excesses and difficulties which always show a tendency to increase at times when we face general elections.

In this way, the Government hopes to be able to achieve a healthy political party system in Indonesia through constitutional and legal means, for the sake of facilitating the running of the wheels of government and to strengthen political stability in the future.

— 3 —

THE POLITICAL ACTION OF THE DEMOCRATIC PARTY OF GUINEA FOR THE EMANCIPATION OF GUINEAN YOUTH

Sékou Touré*

At a time when the greatest confusion prevailed within our youth, the P.D.G. [Democratic Party of Guinea], materialising the unshakeable confidence it never ceased to place in the people, assigned to the young men and women of Guinea a field of activities commensurate with the nation's historic destiny.

To deserve this often reaffirmed confidence, our youth became one of the most active elements of our political revolution. It is not irrelevant to confront the many political, economic, cultural and sporting activities of Guinean youth with the criticisms that were expressed when we decided to unify and democratise its organization.

The rightness of the political line followed in this field by the P.D.G. must help us to strengthen further the cardinal principles on which our political action is founded, constantly improve our organisation, view our goal with always greater accuracy and analyse objectively all new problems directly or indirectly raised by our creative activities.

The J.R.D.A. [Youth of the African Democratic Rally] may not be regarded as a frozen body, with immutable,

* Sékou Touré, *The Political Action of the Democratic Party of Guinea for the Emancipation of Guinean Youth*, 1961, pp. 8, 29-30, 131.

intangible aims. Integrated in the great revolutionary movement of the people of Guinea, the J.R.D.A. must follow the same ascending line as our national revolution's, featured by continuous self-surpassing, uninterrupted progress and a tireless speeding-up of the process of development and evolution of the nation's creative forces. . . .

Officials from the National Political Bureau and the government, and civil servants have expounded to you the new requirements formulated by our party with a view to ensuring a rapid national reconstruction. If the principles taught and the direction given to you are to be of any benefit, it is essential that a certain number of conditions be fulfilled.

The first condition is that you should discern what has been condemned by the Party and as yet is to be found among our social, economic and political realities. You should also discern what has been recommended by the party and as yet is not materialised, thus to be created by our action, in order that the Guinea of tomorrow may be a strong, prosperous nation. Therefore, it is necessary to pick out in our present conditions, the things that are doomed, and those that are called upon to grow as a decisive element for the success of our national revolution. Regression, first and foremost, is condemned, as we choose evolution. *Individualism is condemned, as we have chosen to focus our activities on liberty, solidarity, sovereignty of the people, and not of a few individuals.* Disruptive activities, in direct contradiction to our sacred law of national union, are condemned.

Two categories of trends exist within our society: forces of unity, harmony and understanding, as against the forces of reaction founded upon individualism at the level of the person, parochialism at the level of the tribe or ethnic group, selfishness at the level of the social category. Our party condemns regional parochialism and racialism, it condemns everything undemocratic or counter-revolutionary in nature. Accordingly, *youth must be able to know and to discern, in all aspects of our life, what, by the will of our people, is called to disappear, and what should develop.* Such are the conditions for the liquidation of our current contradictions, which will be achieved through constantly raising the level of our youth's and the whole people's militant conscious-ness.

DIAGRAM OF THE POLITICAL AND ADMINISTRATIVE STRUCTURE OF THE REPUBLIC OF GUINEA

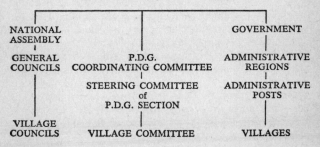

NATIONAL POLITICAL BUREAU
of the
DEMOCRATIC PARTY OF GUINEA

NATIONAL ASSEMBLY		GOVERNMENT
GENERAL COUNCILS	P.D.G. COORDINATING COMMITTEE	ADMINISTRATIVE REGIONS
	STEERING COMMITTEE of P.D.G. SECTION	ADMINISTRATIVE POSTS
VILLAGE COUNCILS	VILLAGE COMMITTEE	VILLAGES

4 — THE CENTRAL SOCIAL AND POLITICAL PROBLEM OF THE U.A.R.—Alan W. Horton*

What groups now give positive support to the new regime? The question is phrased to include the idea of positiveness in order to exclude the apathetic majority, the nonpatriots who are basically neither for nor against any Egyptian government.

The group that springs first to mind is that of the Free Officers, from which has come the nation's new

* Alan W. Horton, "The Central Social and Political Problem of the U.A.R., Part III, The Search for Popular Support," Northeast Africa Series, Vol. IX, No. 4 (United Arab Republic), American Universities Field Staff, Inc., pp. 4-5, 7-11. Reprinted by permission.

leadership. But who are the Free Officers and what is their present relation to those in power? Are they only those officers who demonstrated their convictions by joining the movement prior to 1952, or are they all those who have since shown their loyalty to the regime? To what degree do they now influence public policy? And what officers of both high and low ranks are not Free Officers? To these and other basic questions there are few certain answers. One can say little beyond the obvious fact that there is a group of ex-officers and officers whose interests and predilections have a close relation to central control of the machinery of government, the administration of public enterprise, and the armed power of the state. One can say also that there are some officers whose "reactionary" backgrounds and sentiments have clearly disqualified them from positions of possible political influence.

But the important thing to know about the Free Officers, and about the armed forces at their command, is that they are effectively organized. In the sense that the armed forces are composed of officers and men from all classes of society they are indeed a reflection of Egyptian life; they are separate and distinct, however, in their discipline, orderliness, and ability to act quickly. These are qualities of which Egyptian society stands greatly in need today—and these are the qualities that permit the armed forces, in the face of comparative disorganization elsewhere in the nation, to provide without difficulty a rock-like stability for the regime. In control of the armed forces, the Free Officers—led by Vice-President and Commander in Chief Abd El-Hakim Amer, the President's closest associate—provide positive and dedicated support and receive positions of trust in return.

There is another group, a nonmilitary one, that is equally hard to describe—though for different reasons. It is a group of competent and well-educated men, many of them professionally trained, drawn from various backgrounds toward service to the regime. In its composition the group reflects with reasonable accuracy the amorphousness and fluidity of what President Nasser has recently called the middle classes; it has no social unity beyond that provided by a common allegiance to, and

a common satisfaction with, present policies and programs. . . .

But one searches in vain to discern other groups or
social amalgams that lend positive support to the regime. . . .

The search for positive political support is not essentially a search for stability. Because it is fundamentally
provided by the armed forces, stability is not now one
of the regime's great needs. What is needed is the kind
of mass political institution that can be used by the
regime and its present supporters to effect the psychological and social changes necessary to the emergence of
a nation. What is needed is an institutional beacon that
can attract the apathetic majority and inspire hard work
for patriotic reasons.

The regime has not always been aware of this need.
It has attempted to rally popular support on numerous
occasions, but the purposes have not been clearly thought
out and the necessary institutional maintenance has been
lacking or faulty. By putting some of its ideological tenets
into decree, for example, the regime may have expected
to reap a popularity harvest; if this was indeed the expectation, there was considerable disappointment. The
land-reform law of 1952, which limited private holdings
to 200 feddans, began the job of breaking the power of
the upper class, of establishing a new political climate,
and of righting what was felt to be a great wrong. It did
not, however, provide more than temporary popularity.
The practice of subsidizing the prices of basic foods
demonstrates the regime's belief in economic justice as
well as the desire to keep people from grumbling, but
the sole long-term political result has been a commitment to more of the same. The recently decreed workers'
bonus of 10%, which is in line with the regime's genuine
desire that workers should have a greater share in profits,
is clearly on the way to becoming a rightful expectation
rather than a shining reason for support. None of these
decrees, in other words, has created political capital
available for later investment; none was used for the
building of a new institution.

If decrees have been doubtful political investments,
the same can certainly be said of the appeal of new doc-

trine. Arab socialism and positive neutrality are beguiling concepts only to the few; as political levers to move the mass they are useless without a pedagogical system, an indoctrinating institution. And in the same way a dazzling foreign policy brings few political returns. Though no educated person would deny its effectiveness in finding financial assistance from abroad, present policy has resulted in the sustaining of an uncertain economy but without an increased political appreciation on the part of peasantry and urban poor.

Though the regime has for some time been aware of the importance of building a mass political institution, it has not yet done so effectively. The Liberation Rally of early 1953, though it had other reasons for existence, was declared by Gamal Abdel Nasser, its Secretary General, to be "a means to organize popular strength for the reconstruction of a society on a sound new basis." A basic purpose was clearly to create and regiment the positive popular support needed for rapid change. But the Liberation Rally had other basic purposes as well— and this confusion of purpose certainly contributed to its failure as a mass political institution. A more fundamental cause of failure, however, was the reluctance to allow genuine involvement and responsibility on the part of any but the ruling group.

The same can be said of the National Union, the successor institution established in 1956. Though the National Union has greater singleness of purpose than its predecessor, it has never successfully reconciled retention of regime authority with greater distribution of national responsibility. After the formation of local councils and the establishment of a national structure, it was clear that Union members at all levels were expected to show enthusiasm toward pronouncements and directives from above rather than to express judgments concerning their advisability—in short, to cooperate rather than to consider. The regime now justifies its untrusting attitude toward the rank and file of the National Union by alluding to "reactionary" penetration, a penetration which by inference was partially reflected in the Union-controlled membership of the National Assembly. In a general review of national problems at the Preparatory Committee of the National Congress of Popular Powers on November 25, 1961, President Nasser put it this way: ". . . then reaction began to exploit our interpretation of the National Union, which . . . represents not a party but all the sons and daughters of the country, because we want to gather the whole country with all its classes within the framework of love and national unity. Reaction discovered an opportunity to penetrate into the National Union and to dominate it. . . . In 1960, I felt the revolutionary drive no longer existed. The Revolution began to stumble on capital.". . .

The regime has now publicly recognized that the National Union has not done adequately what it set out to do. Though there have been no recitals of chapter and verse, it is obvious that little has been accomplished in terms of educating the masses to the principles of the Revolution, organizing the masses for rapid change, and fostering social solidarity. In November 1961, at the time of reassessment that followed the defection of Syria, President Nasser implied that the National Union would be reorganized and continued. When he read the Charter for National Action on May 21 of this year, however, it became apparent that even a new name was considered advantageous.

The new political institution is to be known as the Arab Socialist Union. . . .

In the fifth chapter of the Charter, for example, the purposes of the Arab Socialist Union are clearly set forth in terms that might easily have been used in 1956 for the National Union. "There is a dire need to create a new political organization, within the framework of Arab socialist unity, to mobilize the elements capable of leadership, to organize their efforts, to clarify the revolutionary motives of the masses, to sound out their needs and endeavor to satisfy them efficiently.". . .

It is clear that those who stand for election to the Representative Assembly must in some way obtain the approval of the Arab Socialist Union. Less clear are the criteria of Union membership and the power relationships between the Union's leadership and its rank and file.

D. THE ROLE OF THE OPPOSITION

— 1 —

PROBLEMS OF LENINISM
Joseph Stalin*

Therefore, the method of persuasion is the principal method of the Party's leadership of the working class.

"If we, in Russia today," says Lenin, "after two-and-a-half years of unprecedented victories over the bourgeoisie of Russia and the Entente, were to make 'recognition of the dictatorship' a condition of trade-union membership, we should be committing a folly, we should be damaging our influence over the masses, we should be helping the Mensheviks. For the whole task of the Communists is to be able to *convince* the backward elements, to be able to work *among* them, and not to *fence themselves off* from them by artificial and childishly 'Left' slogans."

This, of course, must not be understood in the sense that the Party must convince all the workers, down to the last man, and that only after this is it possible to proceed to action, that only after this is it possible to start operations. Not at all! It only means that before entering upon decisive political actions the Party must, by means of prolonged revolutionary work, secure for itself the support of the majority of the masses of the workers, or at least the benevolent neutrality of the majority of the class. Otherwise Lenin's thesis, that a necessary condition for victorious revolution is that the Party should win over the majority of the working class, would be devoid of all meaning.

* Joseph Stalin, *Problems of Leninism,* 1954, Foreign Languages Publishing House, Moscow, pp. 181-182.

Well, and what is to be done with the minority, if it does not wish, if it does not agree voluntarily to submit to the will of the majority? Can the Party, must the Party, enjoying the confidence of the majority, compel the minority to submit to the will of the majority? Yes, it can and it must. Leadership is ensured by the method of persuading the masses, as the principal method by which the Party influences the masses. This, however, does not preclude, but presupposes, the use of coercion, if such coercion is based on confidence in the Party and support for it on the part of the majority of the working class, if it is applied to the minority after the Party has convinced the majority.

— 2 —

ON THE CORRECT HANDLING OF CONTRADICTIONS AMONG THE PEOPLE, 1957

Mao Tse-tung*

Never has our country been as united as it is today. The victories of the bourgeois-democratic revolution and the socialist revolution, coupled with our achievements in socialist construction, have rapidly changed the face of old China. Now we see before us an even brighter future. The days of national disunity and turmoil which the people detested have gone forever. Led by the working class and the Communist party, and united as one, our 600 million people are engaged in the great work of build-

* Mao Tse-tung, *On the Correct Handling of Contradictions Among the People*, 1957, The New Leader, pp. 14-19. Reprinted by permission.

ing socialism. Unification of the country, unity of the people, and unity among our various nationalities—these are the basic guarantees for the sure triumph of our cause. However, this does not mean that there are no longer any contradictions in our society. It would be naive to imagine that there are no more contradictions. To do so would be to fly in the face of objective reality. We are confronted by two types of social contradictions—contradictions between ourselves and the enemy and contradictions among the people. These two types of contradictions are totally different in nature.

If we are to have a correct understanding of these two different types of contradictions, we must first of all make clear what is meant by "the people" and what is meant by "the enemy."

The term "the people" has different meanings in different countries and in different historical periods in each country. Take our country, for example. During the war of resistance to Japanese aggression, all those classes, strata and social groups which opposed aggression belonged to the category of the people, while the Japanese imperialists, Chinese traitors and the pro-Japanese elements belonged to the category of enemies of the people. During the war of liberation, the United States imperialists and their henchmen—the bureaucrat-capitalists and landlord class—and the Kuomintang reactionaries, who represented these two classes, were the enemies of the people, while all other classes, strata and social groups which opposed these enemies belonged to the category of the people. At this stage of building socialism, all classes, strata and social groups which approve, support and work for the cause of socialist construction belong to the category of the people, while those social forces and groups which resist the socialist revolution, and are hostile to and try to wreck socialist construction, are enemies of the people.

The contradictions between ourselves and our enemies are antagonistic ones. Within the ranks of the people, contradictions among the working people are non-antagonistic, while those between the exploiters and the exploited classes have, apart from their antagonistic aspect, a non-antagonistic aspect. Contradictions among the people have always existed, but their content differs in each period of the revolution and during the building of socialism. . . .

In our country, the contradiction between the working class and the national bourgeoisie is a contradiction among the people. The class struggle waged between the two is, by and large, a class struggle within the ranks of the people; this is because of the dual character of the national bourgeoisie in our country. In the years of the bourgeois-democratic revolution, there was a revolutionary side to their character; there was also a tendency to compromise with the enemy—this was the other side. In the period of the socialist revolution, exploitation of the working class to make profits is one side, while support of the Constitution and willingness to accept socialist transformation is the other. The national bourgeoisie differs from the imperialists, the landlords and the bureaucrat-capitalists. The contradiction between exploiter and exploited which exists between the national bourgeoisie and the working class is an antagonistic one. But, in the concrete conditions existing in China, such an antagonistic contradiction, if properly handled, can be transformed into a non-antagonistic one and resolved in a peaceful way. But if it is not properly handled, if, say, we do not follow a policy of unity, criticizing and educating the national bourgeoisie, or if the national bourgeoisie does not accept this policy, then the contradictions between the working class and the national bourgeoisie can turn into an antagonistic contradiction as between ourselves and the enemy. . . .

Ours is a people's democratic dictatorship, led by the working class and based on the worker-peasant alliance. What is this dictatorship for? Its first function is to suppress the reactionary classes and elements and those exploiters in the country who range themselves against the socialist revolution, to suppress all those who try to wreck our socialist construction; that is to say, to solve the contradictions between ourselves and the enemy within the country—for instance, to arrest, try and sentence certain counter-revolutionaries, and for a specified period of time

deprive landlords and bureaucrat-capitalists of their right
to vote and freedom of speech—all this comes within the
scope of our dictatorship.

— 3 —

TOWARD FREEDOM AND THE DIGNITY OF MAN

President Sukarno*

With regard to the retooling of the political parties, you
already know that Presidential Edict No. 7, 1959, and
Presidential Regulation No. 13, 1960, have come into
force. Presidential Edict No. 7 and Presidential Regulation No. 13 basically in a clear-cut manner give the right
of existence to those parties which adhere to USDEK (of
course, with certain conditions concerning organization,
etc.), and ban those parties which are counter-revolutionary. This is not dictatorship, this is not arbitrary use of
power! This is the application of a universal principle, a
universal principle in any country, namely that one cannot expect the Authorities with whom the power of the
State rests to give the right of existence to forces who
want the downfall of the State, or give weapons, material
or spiritual, to forces who want the downfall of the State.
Added to that, based on revolutionary moral and the
moral of the Revolution, it is the *duty* of the Authorities
to eliminate every force, whether foreign or not, whether
native or not, which endangers the safety or the march of
the Revolution.

Based on these considerations, I now announce to the

* President Sukarno, *Toward Freedom and the Dignity of
   Man,* 1961, Department of Foreign Affairs, Republic of
   Indonesia, pp. 94-95.

People that, in my capacity as President of the Republic of Indonesia—after having heard the opinion of the Supreme Court of Justice—several days ago I ordered the *dissolution of the Masjumi and the P.S.I.* (the Moslem Party Masjumi and the Socialist Party of Indonesia). If one month after the issuance of this order the Masjumi and the P.S.I. have not been dissolved, then these two parties will be *banned parties*.

Do not think that, with this, the Government is hostile to Islam. Yes, indeed, there are persons who are very cunningly insinuating that "Islam is in danger." Such insinuations are criminal, because the Government is not endangering Islam. On the contrary, it extols all religions. The Government takes measures against those *parties* which endanger the State.

You all know that in Presidential Edict No. 7, there is amongst others Article 9, which states:

1) The President, after having heard the Supreme Court of Justice, can ban and/or dissolve a party,

1. which is contrary to the principles and aims of the State;
2. whose programme aims at radically changing the principles and objectives of the State;
3. which is conducting a rebellion because its leaders are taking part in rebellions or have clearly given support to rebellions, while that party has not officially condemned the actions of these members;
4. which do not fulfill the other requirements stipulated in this Presidential Edict.

— 4 —

THE AFRICAN AND DEMOCRACY
Julius Nyerere[*]

I do not think anybody, at this stage of our history, can possibly have any valid reason for claiming that the existence of an Opposition is impossible in an independent African state; but, even supposing this were true, where did the idea of an organization opposition as an essential part of democratic government come from? If one starts, as I have suggested, from the purely etymological definition of democracy it becomes clear that this idea of "for" and "against," this obsession with "Government" balanced by "Official Opposition," is in fact something which, though it *may* exist in a democracy, or *may not* exist in a democracy, is not essential to it, although it happens to have become so familiar to the Western world that its absence immediately raises the cry "Dictatorship."

To the Ancient Greeks, "democracy" meant simply government by discussion. The people discussed, and the result was a "people's government." But not all the people assembled for these discussions, as the textbooks tell us; those who took part in them were "equals" and this excluded the women and the slaves.

The two factors of democracy which I want to bring out here are "discussion" and "equality." Both are essential to it, and both contain a third element, "freedom." There can be no true discussion without freedom, and "equals" must be equal in freedom, without which there

* Julius Nyerere, "The African and Democracy," in *Africa Speaks,* James Duffy and Robert A. Manners (eds.), 1961, D. Van Nostrand Co., Inc., pp. 29-33. Reprinted by permission.

is no equality. A small village in which the villagers are equals who make their own laws and conduct their own affairs by free discussion is the nearest thing to pure democracy. That is why the small Greek state (if one excludes the women and slaves) is so often pointed out to us as "democracy par excellence."

These three, then, I consider to be essential to democratic government: discussion, equality, and freedom—the last being implied by the other two.

Those who doubt the African's ability to establish a democratic society cannot seriously be doubting the African's ability to "discuss." That is the one thing which is as African as the tropical sun. Neither can they be doubting the African's sense of equality, for aristocracy is something foreign to Africa. Even where there is a fairly distinct African aristocracy-by-birth, it can be traced historically to sources outside this continent. Traditionally the African knows no "class." I doubt if there is a word in any African language which is equivalent to "class" or "caste"; not even in those few societies where foreign infiltration has left behind some form of aristocracy is there such a word in the local languages. These aristocrats-by-birth are usually referred to as "the great" or "the clever ones." In my own country, the only two tribes which have a distinct aristocracy are the Bahaya in Buboka, and the Baha in the Buha districts. In both areas the "aristocrats" are historically foreigners, and they belong to the same stock.

The traditional African society, whether it had a chief or not and many, like my own, did not, was a society of equals and it conducted its business through discussion. Recently I was reading a delightful little book on Nyasaland by Mr. Clutton-Brock; in one passage he was describing the life of traditional Nyasa, and when he comes to the Elders he uses a very significant phrase: "They talk till they agree."

"They talk till they agree." That gives you the very essence of traditional African democracy. It is rather a clumsy way of conducting affairs, especially in a world as impatient for results as this of the twentieth century, but discussion is one essential factor of any democracy; and the African is expert at it.

If democracy, then, is a form of government freely established by the people themselves; and if its essentials are free discussion and equality, there is nothing in traditional African society which unfits the African for it. On the contrary, there is everything in his tradition which fits the African to be just what he claims he is, a natural democrat. . . .

Add, then, to the African tradition her lack of an aristocracy and the presence of a moral concept of human dignity on which she is waging her struggle for independence, and place these in the setting of this century of the Declaration of Human Rights, and it becomes difficult to see how anybody can seriously doubt the African's fitness for democracy.

I referred earlier in this article to the "machinery" and the symbols of democratic government. Many of the critics of African democracy are to be found in countries like Britain or the United States of America. These critics, when they challenge our ability to maintain a democratic form of government, really have in mind not democracy but the particular form it has taken in their own countries, the two-party system, and the debate conducted between the Government party and the opposition party within the parliament buildings. In effect, they are saying: "Can you imagine an African Parliament with at least two political parties holding a free debate, one party being 'for' and one 'against' the motion?"

Ghana and Nigeria would be understandably annoyed with me if I were to answer such critics by saying that I *can* "imagine" such countries; for they exist, and they are not figments of my "imagination."

But let us suppose they did not exist. To the Anglo-Saxon in particular, or to countries with an Anglo-Saxon tradition, the two-party system has become the very essence of democracy. It is no use telling an Anglo-Saxon that when a village of a hundred people have sat and talked together until they agreed where a well should be dug they have practiced democracy. The Anglo-Saxon will want to know whether the talking was properly organized. He will want to know whether there was an organized group "for" the motion, and an equally well organized group "against" the motion. He will also want to know whether, in the next debate, the same group will be "for" and the same group "against" the next motion. In other words, he will want to know whether the opposition was organized and therefore *automatic,* or whether it was spontaneous and therefore *free*. Only if it was automatic will he concede that it was democracy!

The new nations of the African continent are emerging today as the result of their struggle for independence. This struggle for freedom from foreign domination is a patriotic one which necessarily leaves no room for difference. It unites all elements in the country so that, not only in Africa but in any other part of the world facing a similar challenge, these countries are led by a nationalist movement rather than by a political party or parties. The same nationalist movement, having united the people and led them to independence, must inevitably form the first government of the new state; it could hardly be expected that a united country should halt in mid-stream and voluntarily divide itself into opposing political groups just for the sake of conforming to what I have called the "Anglo-Saxon form of democracy" at the moment of independence. Indeed, why should it? Surely, if a government is freely elected by the people, there can be nothing undemocratic about it simply because nearly all the people rather than merely a section of them have chosen to vote it into power.

In these circumstances, it would be surprising if the pattern of democracy in Africa were to take—at any rate for the first few years—the shape familiar to Anglo-Saxon countries.

V

THE TOTALITARIAN STATE

Totalitarian dictatorship is a new political phenomenon. It is "historically unique." Its uniqueness lies not so much in any one aspect of the system, for historical parallels can be found for any given factor, but in the combination of the factors which make up the system. Friedrich and Brzezinski describe this combination of factors as follows:

> The basic features or traits we suggest as generally recognized to be common to totalitarian dictatorships are six in number. The "syndrome," or pattern of interrelated traits, of the totalitarian dictatorship consists of an ideology, a single party typically led by one man, a terroristic police, a communications monopoly, a weapons monopoly, and a centrally directed economy. . . .
>
> Neither the Oriental despotisms of the more remote past, nor the absolute monarchies of modern Europe, neither the tyrannies of the ancient Greek cities, nor the Roman Empire, nor yet the tyrannies of the city states of the Italian Renaissance and the Bonapartist military dictatorships of the last century exhibit this design, this combination of features, though they may possess one or another of its constituent parts.[1]

In a separate work Brzezinski discusses the nature of totalitarianism and adds an additional factor to the above syndrome which he considers to be its essence: institutionalized revolutionary zeal. Totalitarianism has been called variously a method, a system, and a process for producing rapid revolutionary change, but one which involves total control over man and society.

The ultimate in control is the technique of thought

[1] C. J. Friedrich and Z. K. Brzezinski, *Totalitarian Dictatorships and Autocracy*, 1956, Harvard University Press, pp. 9-11.

reform (popularly, but erroneously, known as brain washing) used by the People's Republic of China. Historical parallels may be found in certain religious groups such as the Jesuits who have tried in the past to establish specific modes of thought. Furthermore, the Soviet Union has used many of the techniques, especially public confession, which Lifton finds characteristic of thought reform. However, it has been the People's Republic of China that has developed the technique into a system which Lifton calls the "psychology of totalism," and which as a means of control is unique. The required involvement of all adults in study groups and the application of psychological assaults on personality structure may be the progenitor of a new technique of social control.

Within the totalitarian milieu, the institution of the State may be regarded as a means to a specific goal or as an end in itself. Italian fascism considered the State as an end. Mussolini, following Hegel, says: "Fascism conceives of the State as an absolute, in comparison with which all individuals or groups are relative, only to be conceived of in their relation to the State." German fascism preoccupied with racism makes the German "folk" the end for which the State becomes a means. Hitler said specifically: "the state is a means to an end. Its end lies in the preservation and advancement of physically and psychically homogeneous creatures. This preservation itself comprises first of all existence as a race and thereby permits the free development of all forces dormant in this race."

Marxist ideology is dedicated to one concept of the State as a class-linked, transient means to an end. The function of the Communist State is to establish the preconditions necessary to achieve the final end of full communism. It is, in fact, the end or goal-oriented nature of the State that has given communism its "permanent" revolutionary character, which Brzezinski considered essential. The final end of communism is to be achieved by a series of preparatory stages of socialism, each more advanced than its predecessor. The power of the communist leaders as exercised through the State is to a large extent based on the ability to point to satisfactions derived from reaching immediate goals and to the necessity for continuing sacrifices on the part of the people in order to enter the next higher stage. The State acts as the mechanism for this on-going process, but the mechanism will have no further use when full communism is finally attained.

According to Marx and Engels the State is the product of society at a certain stage in its development, the product, more specifically, of the irreconcilability of class antagonism. Its function is the organization of force on the part of the ruling class in order to exploit another class. The bourgeois state suppresses the proletariat, and the proletariat in its turn sets up a dictatorship in order to suppress the remnants of the bourgeoisie. When this is accomplished and a classless society is established, the State, having no further function, will "wither away." Society will then be in the final state of communism in which it will be "to each according to his needs" and only the administering of things will be necessary.

While Marx and Engels set the end and the process or dialectic by which the end was to be achieved, it was left to their successors to wrestle with the problem of determining *when* the State will wither away, a process which presumably would include the liquidation of their own power. This they have been reluctant to do. Lenin gave warning that the withering away of the State would be of a "protracted nature" and that the time span of each preparatory stage must be left open. He also made clear that approach to the final stage would necessitate the increase, not the decrease, of state power. Stalin in 1939 declared that even if a classless, socialist society were achieved within the Soviet Union, full state power would have to be maintained as long as there was capitalist encirclement, that is, until communism was world-wide.

Mao Tse-tung writing in 1949 follows the Marxian thesis in regard to the State, but gives it some specifically Chinese overtones. Reiterating Lenin's theme that much work and sacrifice on the part of the people as well as an accentuation of state power are necessary before the State will die out, Mao says that the people will eventually reach the "realm of Great Harmony," a traditional Confucian concept, but one to be reached by the non-Confucian means of struggle. Furthermore, in the transitional phase the people, and especially the members of the reactionary classes, must be educated and remolded through persuasion by the powerful state apparatus.

Khrushchev's Report on the Program of the Communist Party of the Soviet Union of 1961 is the most advanced communist statement to date on the questions of when and how the final end is to be reached as well as a preliminary tentative sketch of the outlines of the long-awaited stage of full communism. According to Khrushchev the Soviet Union has successfully passed through the first stage of a dictatorship of the proletariat into the more advanced stage of full socialism, and is now entering the third and most advanced stage of socialism which molds and prepares the way for passage into the final goal of communism. The basic distinction between socialism and communism is that in the former rewards are according to work done and in the latter, reward is according to need. For the first time the Program gives a definite timetable. Communism in the Soviet Union will be reached in twenty years. The nature and tasks of the final transitional stage are also laid down. The economy of abundance must be established so that there is sufficient production to provide for each according to his needs. A new Soviet man must be molded who is morally pure, who makes no distinction between rural and urban worker, or physical and mental labor, and who works joyously and selflessly for others. Although the goal of communism is in sight for the Soviet Union, the Report repeatedly emphasizes in the strongest terms that neither state power nor the role of the party will weaken during this transitional stage. Marx to the contrary, Khrushchev says that the State will remain even *after* entering the stage of communism and will take an "entire historical epoch" to wither away. In fact, not unlike Stalin, he hints that this will occur only when the stage of communism has been reached in all countries. The Soviet Union is to be the first to enter communism, but, somewhat ambiguously, all socialist countries are to enter communism at "more or less the same time, within one and the same historical epoch."

However, the Central Committee of the Communist Party of China in a letter to the Central Committee of the Soviet Union in March, 1963, denies that "a state of the whole people," or classless society, can be established prior to the stage of communism. It also denies that the State will exist beyond the stage of socialism, and Khrushchev's statements to the contrary are considered deviations from

Marx-Leninism. It further asserts that all socialist countries "are still far, far removed from the higher stage of
communism." Whether the communist State is projected
into the next stage of communism or is perpetuated for
"a long, long time," the power of the ruling oligarchy as
exercised through the State shows no sign of withering
away.

A. THE NATURE OF TOTALITARIANISM

— 1 —

IDEOLOGY AND POWER IN SOVIET POLITICS

Zbigniew K. Brzezinski*

The crux of any attempted definition of totalitarianism
is the perplexing issue of its uniqueness: What is distinc-
tively new about it? Certainly, autocratic systems in the
past displayed many of the features developed and accen-
tuated by modern totalitarianism. Diocletian's tyranny or
the Shogunate in Japan, for instance, stressed to a high
degree the acquiescence of the population in centralized
control. Both systems also institutionalized an atmosphere
of fear through a system of secret-police informers not
unlike the totalitarian societies of the twentieth century.
Similarly, we find among many of the nineteenth-century
European reformers a readiness to use violence for the
sake of postulated improvements and reforms much like
the ideological intolerance and consequent brutality of the
Rosenbergs or Zhdanovs of our own age. Cromwell's
regime also displayed some analogies. The examples could
easily be multiplied to include many other cases involving

* Zbigniew K. Brzezinski, *Ideology and Power in Soviet
Politics,* Frederick A. Praeger, Inc., 1962, pp. 14-20.
Reprinted by permission.

features similar to some of the characteristics of totalitarianism. Spain is a contemporary example.

Totalitarianism, being a dictatorship, characteristically includes the coercive qualities noted in such varied dictatorial systems. But unlike most dictatorships of the past and present, the totalitarian movements wielding power do not aim to freeze society in the status quo; on the contrary, their aim is to institutionalize a revolution that mounts in scope, and frequently in intensity, as the regime stabilizes itself in power. The purpose of this revolution is to pulverize all existing social units in order to replace the old pluralism with a homogeneous unanimity patterned on the blueprints of the totalitarian ideology. The power of the totalitarian regime is derived not from a precarious balance of existing forces (e.g., church, landed gentry, officer corps), but from the revolutionary dynamism of its zealous supporters, who disarm opposition and mobilize the masses both by force and by an appeal to a better future. This appeal is normally framed in the official ideology, or action program, of the movement. In time, of course, the dynamism decreases, but by then the system is buttressed by complex networks of control that pervade the entire society and mobilize its energies through sheer penetration. An institutionalized revolution, patterned on the totalitarian ideology, thus makes totalitarianism essentially a forward-oriented phenomenon. Most dictatorships, on the other hand, have as their object the prevention of history from keeping in step with time. Their survival depends on maintaining the status quo. When they fail, they become history.

This proposition can be further developed by examining the fate of restraints on political power—which are present in varying degrees in all societies, once the totalitarian movement seizes power. These restraints can be broadly listed in three categories:

1) the direct restraints, expressed through *pacta conventa* such as the English Magna Charta or the Polish *Nihil novi* . . . , the Bill of Rights, constitutional guarantees, a rule of law, or even the broad consensus of tradition that rules out certain types of conduct, such as the use of violence;

2) the indirect restraints that stem from the pluralistic

character of all large-scale societies, necessitating adjustment and compromise as the basis for political power—
e.g., the churches, the economic interests, professional,
cultural, or regional pressure groups, all of which impede
the exercise of unrestrained power; and

3) the natural restraints, such as national character and
tradition, climatic and geographical considerations, kin-
ship structure, and particularly the primary social unit, the
family. These also act to restrain the scope of political
power.

In constitutional societies, all three categories of restraint are operative on political power. In practice, of
course, various violations occur, but these generally constitute a deviation from the norm rather than the norm
itself. Dictatorial or ancient autocratic societies are characterized by the absence of the direct restraints, since
these are incompatible with the nature of arbitrary, and
frequently personal, leadership. Suspension of civil rights,
open or masked subversion of established constitutional
practices, and negation of popular sovereignty have been
characteristic of all nonconstitutional states, whether totalitarian or not.

The indirect restraints, however, have usually escaped
the dictatorial scythe except when a significant social
grouping chooses to resist directly the dictates of those in
power. If, for instance, the church or the nobility, for one
reason or another, clashes with the ruler, it is then subjected to the dictatorial pattern of coercion. Generally,
however, the broad outlines of social life are not disturbed
by the dictator even though an individual objector, even
in a high place, is struck down. An average Hungarian
under Horthy or a Frenchman under Louis XIV was not
directly drawn into the operations of the regime and could
continue in his traditional associations much as before
the advent of the ruler. The ruler himself based his power
to a great extent on the varying alliances reached among
combinations of social-political forces and maintained
himself in power as long as such alliances endured. Revolutionary changes were hence anathema to a dictatorship
of this kind.

It is only totalitarianism of our own age that rejects all
three kinds of restraints. It not only subverts the direct

restraints immediately after the seizure of power but, unlike traditional dictatorships, it proceeds, once entrenched, to destroy all existing associations in society in order to remake that society and, subsequently, even man himself, according to certain "ideal" conceptions. In time, it even attempts, not always successfully, to overcome the natural restraints on political power. Without doing so, totalitarianism can never achieve the isolation of the individual and the mass monolithic homogeneity that are its aim. Only with both of them (the paradox between them is more apparent than real) can the existing pluralism be changed to an active unanimity of the entire population that will make the transformation of society, and ultimately of man, possible. Only through them can man be conditioned to the totalitarian image, for the totalitarian hope is that action patterns will lead to thought patterns. This process, however, even if purposely gradual (as, for instance, in Poland under the Communists), inevitably involves the regime in increasing applications of coercion. Some of the "unredeemable social misfits" have to be removed, and it is difficult for the regime to single out for extinction particular social groups without soon involving itself in large-scale terror. Society is composed, after all, of largely overlapping associations and loyalties. Terror thus becomes an inevitable consequence, as well as instrument, of the revolutionary program. But the totalitarian revolution would be meaningless without a justification to induce the active unanimity of the population. Hence, ideology is not merely a historial guide. It becomes a daily dose of perpetual indoctrination. The total social impact of the totalitarian efforts to make reality conform to totalitarian thought, involving terror and indoctrination as well as institutional and social reorganization, makes for a quantitative difference from old dictatorships that is sufficiently great to become a qualitative difference.

In order to define totalitarianism, one may also attempt to isolate its objective attributes, some of which have already been implied. Carl J. Friedrich suggests that these may include, in a syndrome, the following: an official ideology, a single mass party, a technologically conditioned near-complete monopoly of all means of effective armed combat and of effective mass communication, and a system of terroristic police control. The combination of these by no means exclusively totalitarian characteristics with the total social impact stemming from the inherently dynamic revolutionary spirit of totalitarianism makes it, in terms of the accepted categorizations of political systems, historically distinct. Totalitarianism, therefore, has to be considered as a new form of government falling into the general classification of dictatorship, which includes the ancient autocracies, tyrannies, despotisms, absolute monarchies, and traditional dictatorships. Totalitarianism is a system in which technologically advanced instruments of political power are wielded without restraint by centralized leadership of an elite movement for the purpose of effecting a total social revolution, including the conditioning of man, on the basis of certain arbitrary ideological assumptions proclaimed by the leadership, in an atmosphere of coerced unanimity of the entire population. This definition thus goes beyond Friedrich's descriptive syndrome of discernible characteristics of totalitarianism and attempts to point also to its essence—i.e., its institutionalized revolutionary zeal.

— 2 —

THOUGHT REFORM AND THE PSYCHOLOGY OF TOTALISM

Robert J. Lifton*

Thought reform has a psychological momentum of its own, a self-perpetuating energy not always bound by the interests of the program's directors. When we inquire into

* Robert Jay Lifton, *Thought Reform and the Psychology of Totalism, a Study of "Brainwashing" in China,* 1961, W. W. Norton and Co., Inc., pp. 419-436. Reprinted by permission.

the sources of this momentum, we come upon a complex set of psychological themes, which may be grouped under the general heading of *ideological totalism*. By this ungainly phrase I mean to suggest the coming together of immoderate ideology with equally immoderate individual character traits—an extremist meeting ground between people and ideas. . . .

I wish to suggest a set of criteria against which any environment may be judged—a basis for answering the ever-recurring question: "Isn't this just like 'brainwashing'?"

These criteria consist of eight psychological themes which are predominant within the social field of the thought reform milieu. Each has a totalistic quality; each depends upon an equally absolute philosophical assumption; and each mobilizes certain individual emotional tendencies, mostly of a polarizing nature. Psychological theme, philosophical rationale, and polarized individual tendencies are interdependent; they require, rather than directly cause, each other. In combination they create an atmosphere which may temporarily energize or exhilarate, but which at the same time poses the gravest of human threats.

Milieu Control

The most basic feature of the thought reform environment, the psychological current upon which all else depends, is the control of human communication. Through this milieu control the totalist environment seeks to establish domain over not only the individual's communication with the outside (all that he sees and hears, reads and writes, experiences, and expresses), but also—in its penetration of his inner life—over what we may speak of as his communication with himself. It creates an atmosphere uncomfortably reminiscent of George Orwell's 1984; but with one important difference. Orwell, as a Westerner envisioned milieu control accomplished by a mechanical device, the two-way "telescreen." The Chinese, although they utilize whatever mechanical means they have at their disposal, achieve control of greater psychological depth through a human recording and transmitting apparatus. It is probably fair to say that the Chinese Communist prison and revolutionary university produce about as thoroughly controlled a group environment as has ever existed. The milieu control exerted over the broader social environment of Communist China, while considerably less intense, is in its own way unrivalled in its combination of extensiveness and depth; it is, in fact, one of the distinguishing features of Chinese Communist practice. . . .

For they look upon milieu control as a just and necessary policy, one which need not be kept secret: thought reform participants may be in doubt as to who is telling what to whom, but the fact that extensive information about everyone is being conveyed to the authorities is always known. At the center of this self-justification is their assumption of omniscience, their conviction that reality is their exclusive possession. Having experienced the impact of what they consider to be an ultimate truth (and having the need to dispel any possible inner doubts of their own), they consider it their duty to create an environment containing no more and no less than this "truth." In order to be the engineers of the human soul, they must first bring it under full observational control.

Many things happen psychologically to one exposed to milieu control; the most basic is the disruption of balance between self and outside world. Pressured toward a merger of internal and external milieux, the individual encounters a profound threat to his personal autonomy. He is deprived of the combination of external information and inner reflection which anyone requires to test the realities of his environment and to maintain a measure of identity separate from it. Instead, he is called upon to make an absolute polarization of the real (the prevailing ideology) and the unreal (everything else). To the extent that he does this, he undergoes a *personal closure* which frees him from man's incessant struggle with the elusive subtleties of truth. . . .

He is in either case profoundly hampered in the perpetual human quest for what is true, good, and relevant in the world around him and within himself.

Mystical Manipulation

The inevitable next step after milieu control is extensive personal manipulation. This manipulation assumes a no-

holds-barred character, and uses every possible device at
the milieu's command, no matter how bizarre or painful.
Initiated from above, it seeks to provoke specific patterns
of behavior and emotion in such a way that these will
appear to have arisen spontaneously from within the environment. This element of planned spontaneity, directed
as it is by an ostensibly omniscient group, must assume,
for the manipulated, a near-mystical quality.

Ideological totalists do not pursue this approach *solely*
for the purpose of maintaining a sense of power over
others. Rather they are impelled by a special kind of
mystique which not only justifies such manipulations, but
makes them mandatory. Included in this mystique is a
sense of "higher purpose," of having "directly perceived
some immanent law of social development," and of being
themselves the vanguard of this development. By thus becoming the instruments of their own mystique, they create
a mystical aura around the manipulating institutions—the
Party, the Government, the Organization. They are the
agents "chosen" (by history, by God, or by some other
supernatural force) to carry out the "mystical imperative,"
the pursuit of which must supersede all considerations of
decency or of immediate human welfare. Similarly, any
thought or action which questions the higher purpose is
considered to be stimulated by a lower purpose, to be
backward, selfish, and petty in the face of the great overriding mission. . . .

The Demand for Purity

In the thought reform milieu, as in all situations of
ideological totalism, the experiential world is sharply divided into the pure and the impure, into the absolutely
good and the absolutely evil. The good and the pure are
of course those ideas, feelings, and actions which are
consistent with the totalist ideology and policy; anything
else is apt to be relegated to the bad and the impure.
Nothing human is immune from the flood of stern moral
judgments. All "taints" and "poisons" which contribute
to the existing state of impurity must be searched out and
eliminated.

The philosophical assumption underlying this demand
is that absolute purity (the "good Communist" or the

ideal Communist state) is attainable, and that anything done to anyone in the name of this purity is ultimately moral. In actual practice, however, no one (and no State) is really expected to achieve such perfection. Nor can this paradox be dismissed as merely a means of establishing a high standard to which all can aspire. Thought reform bears witness to its more malignant consequences: for by defining and manipulating the criteria of purity, and then by conducting an all-out war upon impurity, the ideological totalists create a narrow world of guilt and shame. This is perpetuated by an ethos of continuous reform, a demand that one strive permanently and painfully for something which not only does not exist but is in fact alien to the human condition. . . .

People vary greatly in their susceptibilities to guilt and shame (as my subjects illustrated), depending upon patterns developed early in life. But since guilt and shame are basic to human existence, this variation can be no more than a matter of degree. Each person is made vulnerable through his profound inner sensitivities to his own limitations and to his unfulfilled potential; in other words, each is made vulnerable through his existential guilt. Since ideological totalists become the ultimate judges of good and evil within their world, they are able to use these universal tendencies toward guilt and shame as emotional levers for their controlling and manipulative influences. They become the arbiters of existential guilt, authorities without limit in dealing with others' limitations. And their power is nowhere more evident than in their capacity to "forgive.". . .

The Cult of Confession

Closely related to the demand for absolute purity is an obsession with personal confession. Confession is carried beyond its ordinary religious, legal, and therapeutic expressions to the point of becoming a cult in itself. There is the demand that one confess to crimes one has not committed, to sinfulness that is artificially induced, in the name of a cure that is arbitrarily imposed. Such demands are made possible not only by the ubiquitous human tendencies toward guilt and shame but also by the need to give expression to these tendencies. In totalist hands, confession becomes a means of exploiting, rather than offering solace for, these vulnerabilities.

The totalist confession takes on a number of special meanings. It is first a vehicle for the kind of personal purification which we have just discussed, a means of maintaining a perpetual inner emptying or psychological purge of impurity; this *purging milieu* enhances the totalists' hold upon existential guilt. Second, it is an act of symbolic self-surrender, the expression of the merging of individual and environment. Third, it is a means of maintaining an ethos of total exposure—a policy of making public (or at least known to the Organization) everything possible about the life experiences, thoughts, and passions of each individual, and especially those elements which might be regarded as derogatory.

The assumption underlying total exposure (besides those which relate to the demand for purity) is the environment's claim to total ownership of each individual self within it. Private ownership of the mind and its products —of imagination or of memory—becomes highly immoral. . . .

The "Sacred Science"

The totalist milieu maintains an aura of sacredness around its basic dogma, holding it out as an ultimate moral vision for the ordering of human existence. This sacredness is evident in the prohibition (whether or not explicit) against the questioning of basic assumptions, and in the reverence which is demanded for the originators of the Word, the present bearers of the Word, and the Word itself. While thus transcending ordinary concerns of logic, however, the milieu at the same time makes an exaggerated claim of airtight logic, of absolute "scientific" precision. Thus the ultimate moral vision becomes an ultimate science; and the man who dares to criticize it, or to harbor even unspoken alternative ideas, becomes not only immoral and irreverent, but also "unscientific." In this way, the philosopher kings of modern ideological totalism reinforce their authority by claiming to share in the rich and respected heritage of natural science. . . .

Loading the Language

The language of the totalist environment is character-ized by the thought-terminating cliché. The most far-reaching and complex of human problems are compressed into brief, highly reductive, definitive-sounding phrases, easily memorized and easily expressed. These become the start and finish of any ideological analysis. In thought reform, for instance, the phrase "bourgeois mentality" is used to encompass and critically dismiss ordinarily trou-blesome concerns like the quest for individual expression, the exploration of alternative ideas, and the search for perspective and balance in political judgments. And in addition to their function as interpretive shortcuts, these clichés become what Richard Weaver has called "ultimate terms": either "god terms," representative of ultimate good; or "devil terms," representative of ultimate evil. In thought reform, "progress," "progressive," "liberation," "proletarian standpoints" and "the dialectic of history" fall into the former category; "capitalist," "imperialist," "ex-ploiting classes," and "bourgeois" (mentality, liberalism, morality, superstition, greed) of course fall into the latter. Totalist language, then, is repetitiously centered on all-encompassing jargon, prematurely abstract, highly categorical, relentlessly judging, and to anyone but its most devoted advocate, deadly dull: in Lionel Trilling's phrase, "the language of nonthought.". . .

Doctrine Over Person

This sterile language reflects another characteristic feature of ideological totalism: the subordination of hu-man experience to the claims of doctrine. This primacy of doctrine over person is evident in the continual shift be-tween experience itself and the highly abstract interpreta-tion of such experience—between genuine feelings and spurious cataloguing of feelings. It has much to do with the peculiar aura of half-reality which a totalist environ-ment seems, at least to the outsider, to possess. . . . The inspiriting force of such myths cannot be denied; nor can one ignore their capacity for mischief. For when the myth becomes fused with the totalist sacred science, the result-ing "logic" can be so compelling and coercive that it simply replaces the realities of individual experience. Consequently, past historical events are retrospectively altered, wholly rewritten, or ignored, to make them consistent with the doctrinal logic. . . .

The same doctrinal primacy prevails in the totalist approach to changing people: the demand that character and identity be reshaped, not in accordance with one's special nature or potentialities, but rather to fit the rigid contours of the doctrinal mold. The human is thus subjugated to the ahuman. And in this manner, the totalists, as Camus phrases it, "put an abstract idea above human life, even if they call it history, to which they themselves have submitted in advance and to which they will decide quite arbitrarily, to submit everyone else as well.". . .

The Dispensing of Existence

The totalist environment draws a sharp line between those whose right to existence can be recognized, and those who possess no such right. In thought reform, as in Chinese Communist practice generally, the world is divided into the "people" (defined as "the working class, the peasant class, the petite bourgeoisie, and the national bourgeoisie"), and the "reactionaries" or "lackeys of imperialism" (defined as "the landlord class, the bureaucratic capitalist class, and the KMT reactionaries and their henchmen"). Mao Tse-tung makes the existential distinction between the two groups quite explicit:

> Under the leadership of the working class and the Communist Party, these classes [the people] unite together to form their own state and elect their own government [so as to] carry out a dictatorship over the lackeys of imperialism. . . . These two aspects, namely, democracy among the people and dictatorship over the reactionaries, combine to form the people's democratic dictatorship . . . to the hostile classes the state apparatus is the instrument of oppression. It is violent, and not "benevolent.". . . Our benevolence applies only to the people, and not to the reactionary acts of the reactionaries and reactionary classes outside the people.

Being "outside the people," the reactionaries are presumably nonpeople. Under conditions of ideological totalism, in China and elsewhere, nonpeople have often been put to death, their executioners then becoming guilty (in Camus' phrase) of "crimes of logic." But the thought reform process is one means by which nonpeople are permitted, through a change in attitude and personal character, to make themselves over into people. . . .

The more clearly an environment expresses these eight psychological themes, the greater its resemblance to ideological totalism; and the more it utilizes such totalist devices to change people, the greater its resemblance to thought reform (or "brainwashing"). But facile comparisons can be misleading. No milieu ever achieves complete totalism, and many relatively moderate environments show some signs of it. Moreover, totalism tends to be recurrent rather than continuous: in China, for instance, its fullest expression occurs during thought reform; it is less apparent during lulls in thought reform, although it is by no means absent. And like the "enthusiasm" with which it is often associated, totalism is more apt to be present during the early phases of mass movements than later—Communist China in the 1950's was generally more totalist than Soviet Russia. But if totalism has at any time been prominent in a movement, there is always the possibility of its reappearance, even after long periods of relative moderation.

What is the source of ideological totalism? How do these extremist emotional patterns originate? These questions raise the most crucial and the most difficult of human problems. Behind ideological totalism lies the ever-present human quest for the omnipotent guide—for the supernatural force, political party, philosophical ideas, great leader, or precise science—that will bring ultimate solidarity to all men and eliminate the terror of death and nothingness.

B. THE TOTALITARIAN STATE AS END

— 1 —

THE POLITICAL AND SOCIAL DOCTRINE OF FASCISM
Benito Mussolini*

After Socialism, Fascism combats the whole complex system of democratic ideology, and repudiates it, whether in its theoretical premises or in its practical application. Fascism denies that the majority, by the simple fact that it is a majority, can direct human society; it denies that numbers alone can govern by means of a periodical consultation, and it affirms the immutable, beneficial, and fruitful inequality of mankind, which can never be permanently leveled through the mere operation of a mechanical process such as universal suffrage. . . .

The foundation of Fascism is the conception of the State, its character, its duty, and its aim. Fascism conceives of the State as an absolute, in comparison with which all individuals or groups are relative, only to be conceived of in their relation to the State. The conception of the Liberal State is not that of a directing force, guiding the play and development, both material and spiritual, of a collective body, but merely a force limited to the function of recording results: on the other hand, the Fascist State is itself conscious, and has itself a will and a personality—thus it may be called the "ethic" State. In 1929, at the first five-yearly assembly of the Fascist regime, I said:

* Benito Mussolini, "The Political and Social Doctrine of Fascism," *International Conciliation,* No. 315, December 1935, pp. 9-16. Reprinted by permission.

"For us Fascists, the State is not merely a guardian, preoccupied solely with the duty of assuring the personal safety of the citizens; nor is it an organization with purely material aims, such as to guarantee a certain level of well-being and peaceful conditions of life; for a mere council of administration would be sufficient to realize such objects. Nor is it a purely political creation, divorced from all contact with the complex material reality which makes up the life of the individual and the life of the people as a whole. The State, as conceived of and as created by Fascism, is a spiritual and moral fact in itself, since its political, juridical, and economic organization of the nation is a concrete thing: and such an organization must be in its origins and development a manifestation of the spirit. The State is the guarantor of security both internal and external, but it is also the custodian and transmitter of the spirit of the people, as it has grown up through the centuries in language, in customs, and in faith. And the State is not only a living reality of the present, it is also linked with the past and above all with the future, and thus transcending the brief limits of individual life, it represents the immanent spirit of the nation. The forms in which States express themselves may change, but the necessity for such forms is eternal. It is the State which educates its citizens in civic virtue, gives them a consciousness of their mission and welds them into unity; harmonizing their various interests through justice, and transmitting to future generations the mental conquests of science, of art, of law and the solidarity of humanity. It leads men from primitive tribal life to that highest expression of human power which is Empire: it links up through the centuries the names of those of its members who died for its existence and in obedience to its laws, it holds up the memory of the leaders who have increased its territory and the geniuses who have illumined it with glory as an example to be followed by future generations. When the conception of the State declines, and disunifying and centrifugal tendencies prevail, whether of individuals or of particular groups, the nations where such phenomena appear are in their decline." . . .

The Fascist State is an embodied will to power and government: the Roman tradition is here an ideal of force in action. According to Fascism, government is not so much a thing to be expressed in territorial or military terms as in terms of morality and the spirit. It must be thought of as an empire—that is to say, a nation which directly or indirectly rules other nations, without the need for conquering a single square yard of territory. For Fascism, the growth of empire, that is to say the expansion of the nation, is an essential manifestation of vitality, and its opposite a sign of decadence. Peoples which are rising, or rising again after a period of decadence, are always imperialist; any renunciation is a sign of decay and of death.

C. THE TOTALITARIAN STATE AS MEANS

— 1 —

MEIN KAMPF
Adolf Hitler*

Thus the basic realization is: *that the state represents no end, but a means. It is, to be sure, the premise for the formation of a higher human culture, but not its cause, which lies exclusively in the existence of a race capable of culture.* Hundreds of exemplary states might exist on earth, but if the Aryan culture-bearer died out, there would be no culture corresponding to the spiritual level of the highest peoples of today. We can go even farther and say that the fact of human state formation would not in the least exclude the possibility of the destruction of the human race, provided that superior intellectual ability

* The selections from Adolf Hitler, *Mein Kampf* (Ralph Manheim, trans.), 1943, pp. 391-408, are reprinted by permission of and arrangement with Houghton Mifflin Company, the authorized publishers, and the Hutchinson Publishing Group.

and elasticity would be lost due to the absence of their racial bearers.

If today, for example, the surface of the earth were upset by some tectonic event and a new Himalaya rose from the ocean floods, by one single cruel catastrophe the culture of humanity would be destroyed. No state would exist any longer, the bands of all order would be dissolved, the documents of millennial development would be shattered—a single great field of corpses covered by water and mud. But if from this chaos of horror even a few men of a certain race capable of culture had been preserved the earth, upon settling, if only after thousands of years, would again get proofs of human creative power. Only the destruction of the last race capable of culture and its individual members would desolate the earth for good. Conversely, we can see even by examples from the present that state formations in their tribal beginnings can, if their racial supporters lack sufficient genius, not preserve them from destruction. Just as great animal species of prehistoric times had to give way to others and vanish without trace, man must also give way if he lacks a definite spiritual force which alone enables him to find the necessary weapons for his self-preservation.

The *state* in itself does not create a specific cultural level; it can only preserve the race· which conditions this level. Otherwise the state as such may continue to exist unchanged for centuries while, in consequence of a racial mixture which it has not prevented, the cultural capacity of a people and the general aspect of its life conditioned by it have long since suffered a profound change. The present-day state, for example, may very well simulate its existence as a formal mechanism for a certain length of time, but the racial poisoning of our national body creates a cultural decline which even now is terrifyingly manifest.
. . . *Thus, the precondition for the existence of a higher humanity is not the state, but the nation possessing the necessary ability. . . .*

From this the following realization results:

The State is a means to an end. Its end lies in the preservation and advancement of a community of physically and psychically homogeneous creatures. This preservation itself comprises first of all existence as a race and thereby permits the free development of all the forces dormant in this race. Of them a part will always primarily serve the preservation of physical life, and only the remaining part the promotion of a further spiritual development. Actually the one always creates the precondition for the other.

States which do not serve this purpose are misbegotten, monstrosities in fact. The fact of their existence changes this no more than the success of a gang of bandits can justify robbery.

We National Socialists as champions of a new philosophy of life must never base ourselves on so-called 'accepted facts'—and false ones at that. If we did, we would not be the champions of a new great idea, but the coolies of the present-day lie. We must distinguish in the sharpest way between the state as a vessel and the race as its content. This vessel has meaning only if it can preserve and protect the content; otherwise it is useless.

Thus, the highest purpose of a folkish state is concern for the preservation of those original racial elements which bestow culture and create the beauty and dignity of a higher mankind. We, as Aryans, can conceive of the state only as the living organism of a nationality which not only assures the preservation of this nationality, but by the development of its spiritual and ideal abilities leads it to the highest freedom.

But what they try to palm off on us as a state today is usually nothing but a monstrosity born of deepest human error, with untold misery as a consequence.

We National Socialists know that with this conception we stand as revolutionaries in the world of today and are also branded as such. But our thoughts and actions must in no way be determined by the approval or disapproval of our time, but by the binding obligation to a truth which we have recognized. Then we may be convinced that the higher insight of posterity will not only understand our actions of today, but will also confirm their correctness and exalt them. . . .

Anyone who speaks of a mission of the German people on earth must know that it can exist only in the formation of a state which sees its highest task in the preservation and promotion of the most noble elements of our nationality, indeed of all mankind, which still remain intact.

Thus, for the first time the state achieves a lofty inner goal. Compared to the absurd catchword about safeguarding law and order, thus laying a peaceable groundwork for mutual swindles, the task of preserving and advancing the highest humanity, given to this earth by the benevolence of the Almighty, seems a truly high mission.

From a dead mechanism which only lays claim to existence for its own sake, there must be formed a living organism with the exclusive aim of serving a higher idea.

The German Reich as a state must embrace all Germans and has the task, not only of assembling and preserving the most valuable stocks of basic racial elements in this people, but slowly and surely of raising them to a dominant position. . . .

The generation of our present notorious weaklings will obviously cry out against this, and moan and complain about assaults on the holiest human rights. *No, there is only one holiest human right, and this right is at the same time the holiest obligation, to wit: to see to it that the blood is preserved pure and, by preserving the best humanity, to create the possibility of a nobler development of these beings.*

A folkish state must therefore begin by raising marriage from the level of a continuous defilement of the race, and give it the consecration of an institution which is called upon to produce images of the Lord and not monstrosities halfway between man and ape. . . .

Realizing this, the folkish state must not adjust its entire educational work primarily to the inoculation of mere knowledge, but to the breeding of absolutely healthy bodies. The training of mental abilities is only secondary. And here again, first place must be taken by the development of character, especially the promotion of will-power and determination, combined with the training of joy in responsibility, and only in last place comes scientific schooling.

Here the folkish state must proceed from the assumption *that a man of little scientific education but physically healthy, with a good, firm character, imbued with the joy of determination and will-power is more valuable for the national community than a clever weakling.*

— 2 —

STATE AND REVOLUTION
V. I. Lenin*

Summarising his historical analysis Engels says:

The state is therefore by no means a power imposed on
society from the outside; just as little is it "the reality of
the moral idea," "the image and reality of reason," as Hegel
asserted. Rather, it is a product of society at a certain stage
of development; it is the admission that this society has
become entangled in an insoluble contradiction with itself,
that it is cleft into irreconcilable antagonisms which it is
powerless to dispel. But in order that these antagonisms,
classes with conflicting economic interests, may not consume
themselves and society in sterile struggle, a power apparently
standing above society becomes necessary, whose purpose is
to moderate the conflict and keep it within the bounds of
"order"; and this power arising out of society, but placing
itself above it, and increasingly separating itself from it, is
the state.

Here we have, expressed in all its clearness, the basic
idea of Marxism on the question of the historical role
and meaning of the state. The state is the product and
the manifestation of the *irreconcilability* of class antagonisms. The state arises when, where, and to the extent
that the class antagonisms *cannot* be objectively reconciled. And, conversely, the existence of the state proves
that the class antagonisms *are* irreconcilable.

It is precisely on this most important and fundamental

* V. I. Lenin, *State and Revolution*, 1932, International Pub-
    lishers, *passim*. Reprinted by permission.

point that distortions of Marxism arise along two main lines.

On the one hand, the bourgeois, and particularly the petty-bourgeois, ideologists, compelled under the pressure of indisputable historical facts to admit that the state only exists where there are class antagonisms and the class struggle, "correct" Marx in such a way as to make it appear that the state is an organ for *reconciling* the classes. According to Marx, the state could neither arise nor maintain itself if a reconciliation of classes were possible. But with the petty-bourgeois and philistine professors and publicists, the state—and this frequently on the strength of benevolent references to Marx!—becomes a conciliator of the classes. According to Marx, the state is an organ of class *domination,* an organ of *oppression* of one class by another; its aim is the creation of "order" which legalises and perpetuates this oppression by moderating the collisions between the classes. But in the opinion of the petty-bourgeois politicians, order means reconciliation of the classes, and not oppression of one class by another; to moderate collisions does not mean, they say, to deprive the oppressed classes of certain definite means and methods of struggle for overthrowing the oppressors, but to practice reconciliation. . . .

On the other hand, the "Kautskist" distortion of Marx is far more subtle. "Theoretically," there is no denying that the state is the organ of class domination, or that class antagonisms are irreconcilable. But what is forgotten or glossed over is this: if the state is the product of the irreconcilable character of class antagonisms, if it is a force standing *above* society and "increasingly separating itself from it," then it is clear that the liberation of the oppressed class is impossible not only without a violent revolution, *but also without the destruction* of the apparatus of state power, which was created by the ruling class and in which this "separation" is embodied. . . .

Engels' words regarding the "withering away" of the state enjoy such popularity, they are so often quoted, and they show so clearly the essence of the usual adulteration by means of which Marxism is made to look like opportunism, that we must dwell on them in detail. Let us quote the whole passage from which they are taken.

> The proletariat seizes state power, and then transforms the means of production into state property. But in doing this, it puts an end to itself as the proletariat, it puts an end to all class differences and class antagonisms, it puts an end also to the state as the state. Former society, moving in class antagonisms, had need of the state, that is, an organization of the exploiting class at each period for the maintenance of its external conditions of production; therefore, in particular, for the forcible holding down of the exploited class in the conditions of oppression (slavery, bondage or serfdom, wage-labour) determined by the existing mode of production. The state was the official representative of society as a whole, its embodiment in a visible corporate body; but it was this only in so far as it was the state of that class which itself, in its epoch, represented society as a whole: in ancient times, the state of the slave-owning citizens; in the Middle Ages, of the feudal nobility; in our epoch, of the bourgeoisie. When ultimately it becomes really representative of society as a whole, it makes itself superfluous. As soon as there is no longer any class of society to be held in subjection; as soon as, along with class domination and the struggle for individual existence based on the former anarchy of production, the collisions and excesses arising from these have also been abolished, there is nothing more to be repressed, and a special repressive force, a state, is no longer necessary. The first act in which the state really comes forward as the representative of society as a whole—the seizure of the means of production in the name of society—is at the same time its last independent act as a state. The interference of a state power in social relations becomes superfluous in one sphere after another, and then becomes dormant of itself. Government over persons is replaced by the administration of things and the direction of the processes of production. The state is not "abolished," *it withers away*. . . .

The replacement of the bourgeois by the proletarian state is impossible without a violent revolution. The abolition of the proletarian state, *i.e.*, of all states, is only possible through "withering away.". . .

The proletariat needs the state—this is repeated by all the opportunists, social-chauvinists and Kautskyists, who assure us that this is what Marx taught. They "forget," however, to add that, in the first place, the proletariat, according to Marx, needs only a state which is withering away, *i.e.,* a state which is so constituted that it begins to wither away immediately, and cannot but wither away; and, secondly, the workers need "a state, *i.e.,* the proletariat organised as the ruling class."

The state is a special organisation of force; it is the organisation of violence for the suppression of some class. What class must the proletariat suppress? Naturally, the exploiting class only, *i.e.,* the bourgeoisie. The toilers need the state only to overcome the resistance of the exploiters, and only the proletariat can direct this suppression and bring it to fulfilment, for the proletariat is the only class that is thoroughly revolutionary, the only class that can unite all the toilers and the exploited in the struggle against the bourgeoisie, in completely displacing it. . . .

The proletariat needs state power, the centralised organisation of force, the organisation of violence, both for the purpose of crushing the resistance of the exploiters and for the purpose of *guiding* the great mass of the population—the peasantry, the petty-bourgeoisie, the semi-proletarians—in the work of organising Socialist economy. . . .

But the dictatorship of the proletariat—*i.e.,* the organisation of the vanguard of the oppressed as the ruling class for the purpose of crushing the oppressors—cannot produce merely an expansion of democracy. *Together* with an immense expansion of democracy which *for the first time* becomes democracy for the poor, democracy for the people, and not democracy for the rich folk, the dictatorship of the proletariat produces a series of restrictions of liberty in the case of the oppressors, the exploiters, the capitalists. We must crush them in order to free humanity from wage-slavery; their resistance must be broken by force; it is clear that where there is suppression there is also violence, there is no liberty, no democracy.

Engels expressed this splendidly in his letter to Bebel when he said, as the reader will remember, that "as long as the proletariat still *needs* the state, it needs it not in the interests of freedom, but for the purpose of crushing its antagonists; and as soon as it becomes possible to speak of freedom, then the state, as such, ceases to exist." . . .

In other words: under capitalism we have a state in the proper sense of the word, that is, special machinery for the suppression of one class by another, and of the majority by the minority at that. Naturally, for the successful discharge of such a task as the systematic suppression by the exploiting minority of the exploited majority, the greatest ferocity and savagery of suppression are required, seas of blood are required, through which mankind is marching in slavery, serfdom, and wage-labour.

Again, during the *transition* from capitalism to Communism, suppression is *still* necessary; but it is the suppression of the minority of exploiters by the majority of exploited. A special apparatus, special machinery for suppression, the "state," is *still* necessary, but this is now a transitional state, no longer a state in the usual sense, for the suppression of the minority of exploiters, by the majority of the wage slaves of *yesterday*, is a matter comparatively so easy, simple and natural that it will cost far less bloodshed than the suppression of the risings of slaves, serfs or wage labourers, and will cost mankind far less. This is compatible with the diffusion of democracy among such an overwhelming majority of the population, that the need for *special machinery* of suppression will begin to disappear. The exploiters are, naturally, unable to suppress the people without a most complex machinery for performing this task; but *the people* can suppress the exploiters even with very simple "machinery," almost without any "machinery," without any special apparatus, by the simple *organisation of the armed masses* (such as the Soviets of Workers' and Soldiers' Deputies, we may remark, anticipating a little).

Finally, only Communism renders the state absolutely unnecessary, for there is *no one* to be suppressed—"no one" in the sense of a *class*, in the sense of a systematic struggle with a definite section of the population. We are not Utopians, and we do not in the least deny the possibility and inevitably of excesses on the part of *individual persons*, nor the need to suppress *such* excesses. But, in the first place, no special machinery, no special apparatus of repression is needed for this; this will be done by the armed people itself, as simply and as readily as any crowd of civilised people, even in modern society, parts a pair of combatants or does not allow a woman to be outraged. And, secondly, we know that the fundamental social cause of excesses which consist in violating the rules of social life is the exploitation of the masses, their want and their poverty. With the removal of this chief cause, excesses will inevitably begin to *"wither away."* We do not know how quickly and in what succession, but we know that they will wither away. With their withering away, the state will also *wither away.* . . . Marx continues:

> In a higher phase of Communist society, when the enslaving subordination of the individual in the division of labour has disappeared, and with it also the antagonism between mental and physical labour; when labour has become not only a means of living, but itself the first necessity of life; when, along with the all-round development of individuals, the productive forces too have grown, and all the springs of social wealth are flowing more freely—it is only at that stage that it will be possible to pass completely beyond the narrow horizon of bourgeois rights, and for society to inscribe on its banners: from each according to his ability; to each according to his needs!

Only now can we appreciate the full correctness of Engels' remarks in which he mercilessly ridiculed all the absurdity of combining the words "freedom" and "state." While the state exists there is no freedom. When there is freedom, there will be no state. . . .

Consequently, we have a right to speak solely of the inevitable withering away of the state, emphasising the protracted nature of this process and its dependence upon the rapidity of development of the *higher phase* of Communism; leaving quite open the question of lengths of time, or the concrete forms of withering away, since material for the solution of such questions is *not available*.

The state will be able to wither away completely when society has realised the rule: "From each according to his ability; to each according to his needs," *i.e.*, when people have become accustomed to observe the funda-

mental rules of social life, and their labour is so productive, that they voluntarily work *according to their
ability*.

— 3 —

ON THE PEOPLE'S DEMOCRATIC DICTATORSHIP, 1949

Mao Tse-tung*

The first of July 1949 marks the fact that the Communist Party of China has already lived through twenty-
eight years. Like a man, a political party has its childhood, youth, manhood and old age. The Communist
Party of China is no longer a child or a lad in his teens
but has become an adult. When a man reaches old age,
he will die; the same is true of a party. When classes
disappear, all instruments of class struggle—parties and
the state machinery—will lose their function, cease to be
necessary, therefore gradually wither away and end their
historical mission; and human society will move to a
higher stage. We are the opposite of the political parties
of the bourgeoisie. They are afraid to speak of the extinction of classes, state power and parties. We, on the
contrary, declare openly that we are striving hard to
create the very conditions which will bring about their
extinction. The leadership of the Communist Party and
the state power of the people's dictatorship are such conditions. Anyone who does not recognize this truth is no
communist. Young comrades who have not studied Marxism-Leninism and have only recently joined the Party

* Mao Tse-tung, *Selected Works of Mao Tse-tung*, Vol. IV,
    1961, Foreign Languages Press, Peking, pp. 411-412,
    417-419.

may not yet understand this truth. They must understand it—only then can they have a correct world outlook. They must understand that the road to the abolition of classes, to the abolition of state power and to the abolition of parties is the road all mankind must take; it is only a question of time and conditions. Communists the world over are wiser than the bourgeoisie, they understand the laws governing the existence and development of things, they understand dialectics and they can see farther. The bourgeoisie does not welcome this truth because it does not want to be overthrown. To be overthrown is painful and is unbearable to contemplate for those overthrown, for example, for the Kuomintang reactionaries whom we are now overthrowing and for Japanese imperialism which we together with other peoples overthrew some time ago. But for the working class, the labouring people and the Communist Party the question is not one of being overthrown, but of working hard to create the conditions in which classes, state power and political parties will die out very naturally and mankind will enter the realm of Great Harmony. . . .

"You are dictatorial." My dear sirs, you are right, that is just what we are. All the experience the Chinese people have accumulated through several decades teaches us to enforce the people's democratic dictatorship, that is, to deprive the reactionaries of the right to speak and let the people alone have that right.

Who are the people? At the present stage in China, they are the working class, the peasantry, the urban petty bourgeoisie and the national bourgeoisie. These classes, led by the working class and the Communist Party, unite to form their own state and elect their own government; they enforce their dictatorship over the running dogs of imperialism—the landlord class and bureaucrat-bourgeoisie, as well as the representatives of those classes, the Kuomintang reactionaries and their accomplices—suppress them, allow them only to behave themselves and not to be unruly in word or deed. If they speak or act in an unruly way, they will be promptly stopped and punished. Democracy is practised with the ranks of the people, who enjoy the rights of freedom of speech, assembly, association and so on. The right to vote belongs only to the people, not to the reactionaries. The combination of these two aspects, democracy for the people and dictatorship over the reactionaries, is the people's democratic dictatorship.

Why must things be done this way? The reason is quite clear to everybody. If things were not done this way, the revolution would fail, the people would suffer, the country would be conquered.

"Don't you want to abolish state power?" Yes, we do, but not right now; we cannot do it yet. Why? Because imperialism still exists, because domestic reaction still exists, because classes still exist in our country. Our present task is to strengthen the people's state apparatus—mainly the people's army, the people's police and the people's courts—in order to consolidate national defence and protect the people's interests. Given this condition, China can develop steadily, under the leadership of the working class and the Communist Party, from an agricultural into an industrial country and from a new-democratic into a socialist and communist society, can abolish classes and realize the Great Harmony. The state apparatus, including the army, the police and the courts, is the instrument by which one class oppresses another. It is an instrument for the oppression of antagonistic classes; it is violence and not "benevolence." "You are not benevolent!" Quite so. We definitely do not apply a policy of benevolence to the reactionaries and towards the reactionary activities of the reactionary classes. Our policy of benevolence is applied only within the ranks of the people, not beyond them to the reactionaries or to the reactionary activities of reactionary classes.

The people's state protects the people. Only when the people have such a state can they educate and remould themselves on a country-wide scale by democratic methods and, with everyone taking part, shake off the influence of domestic and foreign reactionaries (which is still very strong, will survive for a long time and cannot be quickly destroyed), rid themselves of the bad habits and ideas acquired in the old society, not allow themselves to be led astray by the reactionaries, and continue to advance—to advance towards a socialist and communist society.

Here, the method we employ is democratic, the method of persuasion, not of compulsion. When anyone among the people breaks the law, he too should be punished, imprisoned or even sentenced to death; but this is a matter of a few individual cases, and it differs in principle from the dictatorship exercised over the reactionaries as a class.

As for the members of the reactionary classes and individual reactionaries, so long as they do not rebel, sabotage or create trouble after their political power has been overthrown, land and work will be given to them as well in order to allow them to live and remould themselves through labour into new people. If they are not willing to work, the people's state will compel them to work. Propaganda and educational work will be done among them too and will be done, moreover, with as much care and thoroughness as among the captured army officers in the past. This, too, may be called a "policy of benevolence" if you like, but it is imposed by us on the members of the enemy classes and cannot be mentioned in the same breath with the work of self-education which we carry on within the ranks of the revolutionary people.

Such remoulding of members of the reactionary classes can be accomplished only by a state of the people's democratic dictatorship under the leadership of the Communist Party. When it is well done, China's major exploiting classes, the landlord class and the bureaucrat-bourgeoisie (the monopoly capitalist class), will be eliminated for good. There remain the national bourgeoisie; at the present stage, we can already do a good deal of suitable educational work with many of them. When the time comes to realize socialism, that is, to nationalize private enterprise, we shall carry the work of educating and remoulding them a step further. The people have a powerful state apparatus in their hands—there is no need to fear rebellion by the national bourgeoisie.

— 4 —

REPORT ON THE PROGRAM OF THE COMMUNIST PARTY OF THE SOVIET UNION, 1961

N. S. Khrushchev*

Comrades, the Twentieth Congress instructed the Central Committee to draft a new Program of the Communist Party of the Soviet Union. The Central Committee has done so, and submits the draft, after it has been discussed by the Party and the people, to the Congress for consideration.

Our Congress will go down in history as the congress of the builders of communism, the congress that considered and adopted the great program for the building of the first communist society in the history of mankind. . . .

In their struggle the working class and its Communist Party go through three historic stages of world impact —overthrow of the rule of the exploiters and establishment of the dictatorship of the proletariat, construction of socialism, moulding of a communist society.

Our Party and people have accomplished the first two stages. And the fact that the Party was invariably successful in each of these stages is due, to a very great extent, to its having a true compass—its militant revolutionary Party programs built upon the granite foundation of Marxism-Leninism. . . .

* Documents of the 22nd Congress of the CPSU, Vol. II, N. S. Khrushchev, *Report on the Program of the Communist Party of the Soviet Union,* October 17, 1961, Cross Currents Press, *passim.* Reprinted by permission.

The historical limits of the draft Program are 20 years. Why did we set this term? When the draft Program was being discussed, some comrades wondered whether the time allocated to the task was not too long. No, comrades. To prepare society for the principles of communism we have to develop the productive forces enormously and create an abundance of material and spiritual values. And that takes a certain amount of time. The bowl of communism is a bowl of abundance that must always be full. Everyone must contribute his bit to it, and everyone must take from it.

It would be a fatal error to decree the introduction of communism before all the necessary conditions for it have matured. If we were to proclaim that we introduce communism when the bowl is still far from full, we would be unable to take from it according to needs. In that case we would only discredit the ideas of communism, disrupt the initiative of the working people and retard the advance to communism. We base ourselves on strictly scientific estimates, which indicate that we shall, in the main, have built a communist society within 20 years.

What does it mean to build communism in the main? It means that: in the *economic* sphere the material and technical basis of communism will be created, the Soviet Union will surpass the economic level of the most developed capitalist countries and move into first place for production per head of the population, the world's highest living standard will be ensured, and all the preconditions created to attain an abundance of material and cultural values; in the sphere of *social* relations the still existing distinctions between classes will be eliminated; classes will fuse into a classless society of communist working people; the essential distinctions between town and country, and then between physical and mental labor, will, in the main, be eradicated; there will be greater economic and ideological community among nations; the features of the man of communist society will develop, harmoniously combining ideological integrity, broad education, moral purity and physical perfection; in the *political* sphere all citizens will participate in the administration of public affairs, and society will prepare itself for the full implementation of the principles of communist self-government through a most extensive development of socialist democracy. . . .

With the victory of socialism and the country's entry into the period of full-scale communist construction, the working class of the Soviet Union has on its own initiative, consistent with the tasks of communist construction, transformed the state of proletarian dictatorship into a state of the whole people. That, comrades, is a fact unparalleled in history! Until now the state has always been an instrument of dictatorship by this or that class. In our country, for the first time in history, a state has taken shape which is not a dictatorship of any one class, but an instrument of society as a whole, of the entire people.

Communist construction no longer requires the dictatorship of the proletariat. All working people in our society have equal rights. To be sure, the working class continues to play the leading role in society also during the transition to communism. It retains this role, because it is the most advanced class, the most organized, a class associated with machine industry, one that is the most consistent bearer of communist ideals. . . .

But why, for all that, is the state as such being retained, though the antagonism of classes, the main thing that gave rise to it, has disappeared? It is being retained because the tasks which society can solve only with the aid of the state are not as yet consummated. These purposes and functions of the socialist state are defined conclusively in the draft of our Party Program.

The state will remain long after the victory of the first phase of communism. The process of its withering away will be a very long one; it will cover an entire historical epoch and will not end until society is completely ripe for self-government. For some time, features of state administration and public self-government will intermingle. In this process the domestic functions of the state will develop and change, and gradually lose their political character. It is only after a developed communist society is built up in the U.S.S.R., and provided socialism wins and consolidates in the international arena, that there will no longer be any need for the state, and it will wither away. . . .

— 5 —

THE GENERAL LINE OF THE INTERNATIONAL COMMUNIST MOVEMENT, 1963

Central Committee of the Communist Party of China*

Both Marx and Lenin maintained that the entire period before the advent of the higher stage of communist society is the period of transition from capitalism to communism, the period of the dictatorship of the proletariat. In this transition period, the dictatorship of the proletariat, that is to say, the proletarian state, goes through the dialectical process of establishment, consolidation, strengthening and withering away.

In the *Critique of the Gotha Program,* Marx posed the question as follows:

> Between capitalist and communist society lies the period of the revolutionary transformation of the one into the other. There corresponds to this also a political transition period in which the state can be nothing but *the revolutionary dictatorship of the proletariat.*

Lenin frequently emphasized Marx's great theory of the dictatorship of the proletariat and analysed the de-

* "A Proposal Concerning the General Line of the International Communist Movement," a Letter of the Central Committee of the Communist Party of China in reply to the Central Committee of the Communist Party of the Soviet Union of March 30, 1963. *Peking Review,* No. 30, July 26, 1963, pp. 20-21.

velopment of this theory, particularly in his outstanding work, *The State and Revolution,* where he wrote:

> . . . the transition from capitalist society—which is developing toward communism—to a communist society is impossible without a "political transition period," and the state in this period can only be the revolutionary dictatorship of the proletariat.

He further said:

> The essence of Marx's teaching on the state has been mastered only by those who understand that the dictatorship of a *single* class is necessary not only for every class society in general, not only for the *proletariat* which has overthrown the bourgeoisie, but also for the entire *historical period* which separates capitalism from "classless society," from communism.

As stated above, the fundamental thesis of Marx and Lenin is that the dictatorship of the proletariat will inevitably continue for the entire historical period of the transition from capitalism to communism, that is, for the entire period up to the abolition of all class differences and the entry into a classless society, the higher stage of communist society.

What will happen if it is announced, halfway through, that the dictatorship of the proletariat is no longer necessary?

Does this not fundamentally conflict with the teachings of Marx and Lenin on the state of the dictatorship of the proletariat?

Does this not license the development of "this contagion, this plague, this ulcer that socialism has inherited from capitalism"?

In other words, this would lead to extremely grave consequences and make any transition to communism out of the question.

Can there be a "state of the whole people"? Is it possible to replace the state of the dictatorship of the proletariat by a "state of the whole people"?

This is not a question about the internal affairs of any particular country but a fundamental problem involving the universal truth of Marxism-Leninism.

In the view of Marxist-Leninists, there is no such thing as a non-class or supra-class state. So long as the state remains a state, it must bear a class character; so long as the state exists, it cannot be a state of the "whole people." As soon as society becomes classless, there will no longer be a state.